MORE PRECIOUS THAN
SILVER

Ps. 45:1

MORE PRECIOUS THAN
SILVER

THE GOD STORIES BEHIND THE SONGS OF LYNN DESHAZO

LYNN DESHAZO
FOREWORD BY DON MOEN

WinePress Publishing (PO Box 428, Enumclaw, WA 98022) functions only as book publisher. As such, the ultimate design, content, editorial accuracy, and views expressed or implied in this work are those of the author.

Unless otherwise noted, all Scriptures are taken from the *New American Standard Bible*, © 1960, 1963, 1968, 1971, 1972, 1973, 1975, 1977, 1995 by The Lockman Foundation. Used by permission.

ISBN 13: 978-1-60615-018-4
ISBN 10: 1-60615-018-9
Library of Congress Catalog Card Number: 2009932470

To Dr. Shirley Arnold,
with gratitude and much affection

CONTENTS

ACKNOWLEDGMENTS

I know something about writing a song. But, to parody a line from the movie *Gone with the Wind*, I must confess that "I don't know nuthin' 'bout writin' books!"

I knew from the start that I needed an editor. As God would have it, one happened to contact me while I was just beginning the first few chapters. An author and speaker named Eva Marie Everson sent me an e-mail message requesting background information for an article she was writing about "More Precious Than Silver" (I've since learned that writers are always doing stuff like that). I helped her with her questions, proofed the article she was writing for accuracy, and asked if I might contact her later. I was in the early stages of writing a book, I said, and wondered if she could perhaps suggest to me the names of some editors.

"Me!" she wrote right back, and I had my editor. She's a really good one, by the way. Thank you, Eva, for all your hard work and for your friendship. This book definitely would not be what it is without you!

Thank you, Don Moen, for agreeing to write the foreword. You are such a respected voice among worship ministers and church leaders around the globe. I appreciate your willingness to speak on my behalf.

Many thanks go to the good people at Integrity Music, who have published my songs and faithfully administered my catalog for over twenty years. I am honored to be a partner in your mission to "help people worldwide experience the manifest presence of God." Thank you for permission to reprint all the song lyrics.

Thank you, Gary Sadler, for your permission as cowriter to reprint "There's a Table." You are always such a joy to write with.

Thank you, Freddie and Mary Ann Piro at Dunamis Music, for your kind permission to quote from the lyrics of Love Song's "Praise the Lord."

Thank you, Valeta Bush, for your gracious permission to reprint Ms. Ev's eulogy. Her life still speaks volumes to me about the love of God, and so does yours!

I want to thank the people at Liberty Church, especially the "Bagley Bunch," for their faithful prayers for me and for this book. You have helped give wings to my words!

Thanks to Clay and Mary McLean for taking time to read the manuscript, for your generous encouragement, your friendship, and your prayers. Clay, your ministry has impacted my life and writing more than you'll ever know. I know that I have drawn on your teaching both consciously and unconsciously for this book.

I want to especially thank my biggest fans—my parents, Tom and Bettie DeShazo. There would be no story to tell at all without you! And thanks to my other biggest fans—my brothers, Tommy and Jeff; and nephew, Samuel. You are my best encouragers.

Myriads of people in my life are also deserving of sincere thanks. God knows who you are, and He will reward you.

FOREWORD

I've always had the greatest respect and most genuine admiration for songwriters. As a boy, I spent countless hours listening to their stories embedded in lyrics sung by some of the greatest artists of the mid-twentieth century.

I never thought much about pursuing a career in songwriting as a kid, but I loved a great melody, and melodies seemed to come easily to me. My family had a tiny lake cottage in northern Minnesota, where we spent a good part of each summer. The cottage (an old railroad shack that leaked like a sieve) was so small that when one person went to bed, everyone had to go to bed! In the mornings as we lay there, not able to get up until everyone got up, my mother used to sing spontaneous, silly songs about each of her four kids. Hilarious!

Eventually, during college I began touring with a musical group, and out of sheer desperation for some new repertoire, I took a crack at writing my first song. Unfortunately, it sounded very similar to those songs my mother used to make up!

Now, after many years as a songwriter, I appreciate just how much of a challenge there is to making a certain lyric and a certain melody seem as if they were meant for each other. Certainly, some innate ability is a plus in writing compelling and memorable songs, but I've found that one thing differentiates great songwriters from good songwriters: great songwriters work harder and longer than good writers. And that dedication is the first quality that makes Lynn DeShazo a great writer.

My friend told me a story about meeting the legendary songwriter Sammy Cahn. Sammy wrote many of Frank Sinatra's big hits. He asked my friend, "What comes first when you are writing a song, the lyric or the melody?"

While my friend was thinking, Sammy said, "The answer is neither. The phone call comes first: 'Sammy, we have Frank in the studio, and we need a big song . . . *now!*'"

The world is still singing Sammy Cahn songs, so I think we can safely say that he responded to the pressure of the moment and the demand on his gift, creating something of lasting beauty. Great songwriters do that.

While a popular songwriter's job is to help an artist tell a story that his or her audience will find compelling, it is the responsibility of the worship songwriter not to serve the artist but to put words in the mouths of worshippers. The goal of the worship writer isn't to advance the plot of a musical or provide an artist with a vehicle for his artistry, but to give God's creation a language and a means of expression to approach the divine and express the full range of human emotions to the triune God. What an incredible and awesome responsibility!

To be a great worship songwriter, you need to know whom you are writing about. You can't talk about God in some abstract, theoretical way. Instead, you need to know Him intimately as a son or daughter, as a friend, or perhaps even as a lover. This, then, brings us again to my friend Lynn DeShazo.

Lynn knows of what she writes. She has spent a lifetime passionately pursuing God, getting to know her King, Creator, Savior, Redeemer, and Friend. It is out of this devotion that songs such as "More Precious Than Silver," "Ancient Words," "Be Magnified," and dozens of others have sprung. The Holy Spirit continues to put a demand on Lynn DeShazo's gift. When Lynn marries great lyrics to great melody in ways that allow you and me to enter into God's presence, she is enabling us to do something we will do for all eternity—worship our Creator.

More Precious Than Silver is more than a compilation of "moving stories behind extraordinary songs." While Lynn's stories are compelling, I found this book to be so much more than a glimpse into the songwriting process of one of today's most prolific worship writers. This is a touching, inspiring, personal testimony of how God met Lynn in her darkest hour and has proved Himself faithful—again and again.

This book moved me, and I know it will move you too.

—Don Moen
Worship leader, music executive, and songwriter
Nashville, Tennessee
July 2009

CHAPTER ONE

MORE PRECIOUS
THAN SILVER

For who has despised the day of small things?
—Zechariah 4:10

When you see my name, Lynn DeShazo, bells probably won't go
off. There most likely won't be any moments of "Oh, yeah, I
know her!" But what you may recognize, if you've spent any time in
churches with "contemporary" song services, is a song I wrote titled
"More Precious Than Silver." Because of its enduring popularity over
the last thirty years, I actually consider it my "claim to fame" song. A
line from the chorus even made it into the pages of *Reader's Digest* as a
church bulletin blooper. "Lord, You are more costly than *gold*" became
"Lord, You are more costly than *golf!*"

Even after all these years, I can't explain why this song is still on the
radar screen of songs the church is singing, but I am grateful it is, for
whatever the reason. That little song has opened a lot of doors for me.

In the 1980s, as the song began to gain popularity among churches
experiencing spiritual renewal, I was inevitably asked about how
it came to be written. Along the way, an article or two appeared in
worship ministry periodicals, and the story continues to be told today
as new books are written about the church's popular worship songs.
Those articles and books tell the story from my early perspective, and if
you've read any of them and you're even mildly curious, the answer is

yes! It's really true that McDonald's french fries and fasting played a big role in the writing of what would become a classic worship song.

When I was in the fourth grade, I received my first guitar for Christmas. I started lessons soon afterward at age eleven and continued them for about three and a half years. I was musical; I progressed quickly and easily picked out the chords to a lot of the pop songs I heard on the radio. I even put together a makeshift garage band with some of the neighborhood kids. We were all just learning to play our individual instruments and had grand delusions of becoming rock stars. I'm sure now that we sounded just terrible, but it was still great fun. It also gave me my initial understanding of how words and music become songs.

As I grew a little older, my musical influences began to include a lot more singers-songwriters than bands. I loved the music of James Taylor, Simon and Garfunkel, Jim Croce, John Denver, Gordon Lightfoot, and others like them. I also admit to owning every album Creedence Clearwater Revival ever put out. Well, except *Mardi Gras*.

If I heard it on the radio and liked it, whatever the song, I attempted to play it.

You don't need a formal education in music to be a songwriter, but you *do* need to have a knack for putting words and music together. All my hours of listening and emulating played an important role in my early development as a songwriter.

Another place where I honed my skills was in my Girl Scout troop. At least five of us played guitars; during weekend camping events—which meant a campfire—the guitars came out in full force. We spent many hours playing and singing the folk songs that were circulating at the time—songs like "If I Had a Hammer" and "500 Miles"—as well as our current radio favorites. I always thought we did a pretty mean rendition of "Dead Skunk in the Middle of the Road"!

When the Holy Spirit began to move in a fresh way during the Jesus Movement of the late 1960s and early 1970s, He touched young people who began to use the music they loved and were beginning to create for themselves to reach their generation with the good news. This time spawned a lot of simply written yet powerful new songs of praise and worship in the church.

I can still remember the first time I heard a worship song from Maranatha! Music's *The Praise Album* play over the radio as I drove my parents' car.

> Praise the Lord, praise the Lord!
> Praise to Jesus Christ from Whom all blessings flow!
> Let's open up our hearts,
> Let the living water give our lives a start.[1]

Something in that music absolutely captured my heart. Today, of course, I understand it was the anointing of the Holy Spirit on the music offered as worship. At the time, I just knew I had to have that music. It was full of life! I think, too, that the experience set a kind of standard for me about the songs I would eventually go on to write.

I started writing songs in high school that I'll simply refer to as "Christian." Some of these took the form of testimony, and others were Scripture inspired or simple expressions of worship. I wrote almost more by accident than by any focused effort to sit down and compose. In fact, once I started my college education, I think I wrote only about three songs a year for the first three years. I was, however, willing to share what I had when opportunities arose, such as in my work with a Presbyterian youth group, as a camp counselor, and as a dorm devotional giver. I found that the songs evoked positive responses from my friends who heard them, and this affirmation encouraged me to do more.

When I began my studies at Auburn University as a pre-pharmacy student, I had no clear idea of what I wanted to do in life. I don't even know why I picked that program, other than, I think, that it looked like something I could do.

My dad tried to talk me out of it. He said, "Have you ever gone down to a drugstore and watched what they do all day?"

He was right, of course; a career in pharmacy was not the road for me. I had so much trouble with the chemistry requirements that I took most of those courses twice. Facing reality, along with the suggestion of a scouting buddy, I changed my major to recreation administration. My grades vastly improved, and I started making the dean's list. In the summer of 1978—my senior year—I worked in my professional internship with a city parks and recreation program near my home in Birmingham, Alabama. That fall I returned to the Auburn campus for my last quarter of academic classes.

That period of completing one's education and preparing to enter the "real world" is a scary time for most young adults. It's exciting, of course, but also a bit daunting. It was no different for me. As I neared the end of my time at Auburn, I started praying in earnest about the direction and plans God had for my life. In the meantime a new campus ministry, Bob Weiner's Maranatha Campus Ministries, had started a new chapter at Auburn, and I decided to check out its outreach meetings.

The leaders preached a radical message of total commitment to Christ, which got my attention. I needed a sense of purpose for my life, and the ministry emphasis appealed to me. I became part of the fledgling campus church. I was discipled and ministered to in a way I'd never experienced before. I loved the emphasis on praising the Lord and received some good foundational teaching on biblical worship. Eventually, plans were made to form a praise and worship team, and a call went out to "bring your instruments to the next meeting if you are interested in being a part of it." By this time, I had written a number of songs and was accustomed to singing and playing them for friends and Christian groups I'd been involved with, so I was eager to try out.

My musical talent had become my primary source of affirmation in life. I enjoyed plenty of other things, such as athletics and other recreational pursuits, but music was and is where I stood out. Although I had a lot of deep-seated insecurities about myself, being able to play guitar and write songs made them bearable. Standing behind my guitar, both literally and figuratively, was like wearing a suit of armor. When I composed and played, I felt affirmed and accepted, and even protected. That I could play guitar and sing my songs for the Lord also gave me a sense of being approved by Him.

"Surely the Lord must be pleased with me as long as I can do this for Him," I told myself.

Performance orientation was a strong undercurrent in my life, a need to please others in order to win approval and affirmation from authority figures—and consequently, from God. My anxiety to "get it right" ran high, especially concerning spiritual things. Sometimes I think that tendency comes from being a firstborn child; firstborns often develop an acute sense of responsibility. Whatever the reason, I clung to my music like a drowning man clings to whatever he can hold onto to keep his head above water. From the time I learned how to play, my guitar had become practically an appendage to my body.

When the next meeting of the campus ministry rolled around, I was there with my guitar clutched firmly in my hand. Before the praise team auditions took place, however, we had our regular service of worship and preaching. The text of the sermon was from Exodus 33:6: "So the sons of Israel stripped themselves of their ornaments, from Mount Horeb onward."

I can't remember a single word the preacher said to the group that night, but I remember the message the Holy Spirit preached to me as if it were yesterday.

"I want your guitar."

Excuse me?

"I want your guitar."

Now, I could have argued with God all night, but there was no mistaking what I'd just heard in my heart: *"I want you to give up your guitar."*

I'm sure all the color drained from my face as I struggled with what I knew the Lord was asking me to do. Struggle or not, how could I profess to belong to God and not obey Him when He spoke to me? Finally, with tears streaming down my face, I laid down the guitar.

At the close of the meeting, I tearfully spoke to my pastor about what God had said to me and about what I had to do. I asked him if he'd hang on to my guitar for a while. Graciously, he agreed; it stayed under his bed for several months as the Lord took me through a necessary process. I had come to rely on what I could do for God as my security before Him, and God, because He loved me, would not allow that to go on any longer. I had come to my personal Mount Horeb.

Although many of my friends at college were dismayed that I'd put aside my guitar, it was during those months that I began learning how to lean on Christ alone for my security and for my approval in the

Father's eyes. I stood and worshipped in the congregation with everyone else while others played their instruments and led the praises of God. As the fall quarter drew to a close, I completed my exams, graduated from Auburn University, and returned home for the holidays. I had decided to continue with the ministry, so I returned to Auburn the following January to live and find work.

Auburn, being a small town, offered few opportunities for recent graduates and none in my field. But there *was* a McDonald's within walking distance of where I lived, so I applied for a job there and got it. That's right; I ended up doing the one thing every parent hopes his or her child will avoid after earning a degree from a four-year institution of higher learning—I sold burgers and fries!

Aside from the fact that I had no car and little money and that my parents thought I had joined a cult, this was a good season of life for me. I was excited about what I was experiencing in my personal relationship with Christ and about being part of a dynamic ministry. I was being stretched daily in my understanding of what it meant to be a disciple of Jesus, which included learning about the discipline of prayer and fasting.

Every so often our pastor called us to a day of fasting, which concluded with the church coming together for a time of intercessory prayer. Fasting was a whole new experience for me, and I found it quite a challenge to go all day without eating, made more difficult on the days I worked a shift at McDonald's.

It's amazing how much you think about food when you're not supposed to be eating any. And, if you happen to be in charge of the french fry station at a fast-food restaurant while you're attempting to fast, it's nearly impossible! Those delicious, mouthwatering, golden fries that McDonald's is so famous for were staring me in the face at all times. Shoot, they were hard to resist even on days when I *wasn't* fasting! Then came one particular July day when the fries won the battle, hands down. And when I say "hands down," what I mean is that my hands went down into the bin and came up with about two or three fries. After checking to make sure no one was watching, I popped the forbidden fruit into my mouth.

For about five seconds I felt energized by the food. Then a cloud of condemnation settled on me.

Some kind of a Christian you are, my mind assailed. *You couldn't even get through one day of fasting without caving in early,* it shouted.

I felt miserable for my fasting failure. At the end of my shift, I walked home with a heavy heart. I could have easily wallowed in self-pity, but instead of allowing the condemnation to keep me away from the Lord, I went to Him and worshipped, most certainly with repentance. I sat on the edge of my bed and pulled my guitar from its case (by this time the Lord had released me to play again), opened my Bible, and began singing to Him. My heart was soon flooded with a sense of His presence. Spontaneously, I began to sing a new song.

> Lord, You are more precious than silver,
> Lord, You are more costly than gold,
> Lord, You are more beautiful than diamonds,
> And nothing I desire compares with You.

I was electrified by what I was experiencing. I felt the wonderful, loving presence of Jesus in an extraordinary way. I realized that I was singing words to Him that I'd never heard before. I had written songs in the past but never quite like this! This song was flowing from a river of living water within me. It came from a place of rest in God, not out of the old broken place of striving to please Him. This was a new day for me. It was also the first song I'd written since God had called me to lay down my instrument almost ten months earlier.

Two Scripture verses seemed to merge themselves as I sang. I recalled Colossians 2:3, which says that hidden in Christ is "all the treasures of wisdom and knowledge," and Proverbs 8:11, which states, "For wisdom is better than jewels; and all desirable things cannot compare with her."

I worked on the song over the next few days. After I shared it with the worship leader of our church, we sang it regularly in our worship services. A couple of weeks later, I thought the song needed something more, so I wrote a bridge section that people are still surprised to learn about today.

One of the women of our church shared the chorus with her brother, who worked with the music ministry of Christ for the Nations Institute (CFNI) in Dallas, Texas. He liked the song and, soon after hearing it, taught it to the student body, which resulted in it being recorded by the CFNI students on a live worship tape. (This was in the early 1980s.)

Although I was unaware of it at the time, "More Precious Than Silver" was actually published among the nations of the world through CFNI efforts. I soon received regular correspondence from individuals and from churches, requesting permission to use the song in their worship services. All the while, I had no idea how they even knew about the song. I was just in awe of what God was doing, which was quite apart from my personal efforts to make it known.

As I said earlier, "More Precious Than Silver" has opened a lot of doors for me over the years. One of the first was what would become a long-term publishing relationship with Integrity Music. (The year 2009 marked my twentieth year with them.) A number of the songs I've written have appeared on the various Hosanna! Music worship recordings Integrity Music has produced since the company began in the mid-1980s. Because the product is distributed widely throughout the world, my songs have enjoyed a global audience through Integrity's efforts.

In 2006 during my last trip overseas, a very kind Nigerian pastor in Lagos introduced me to his church by mentioning a few of the songs I had written. When he said, "More Precious Than Silver," a wave of delighted "oohs" ran across the large congregation as they expressed their appreciation with enthusiasm.

To be honest, I never grow tired of those moments; across the world and right here at home, it's still amazing to hear people singing "More Precious Than Silver" along with me.

Even after all these years.

We are, at the time of the writing of this book, experiencing a worldwide financial downslide. Markets are swinging wildly on a daily basis. Every appearance suggests that we have entered a time of global recession. In the United States, as the mortgage and credit crisis continues almost unabated, the housing market is practically lifeless. Trillions of dollars of paper wealth have disappeared overnight, and with them have disappeared a lot of the future dreams of individual investors. To paraphrase the words of Jesus, "Thieves have broken in" and "All manner of moths and rust have destroyed" (Matt. 6:19).

I am reminded of more of His words: that where our treasure is, there will our hearts be also. It strikes me that now would be an excellent time for us to examine our hearts afresh and perhaps discover where our treasure really lies.

What has your heart, friend? Or, more importantly, who?

Care to sing along?

More Precious Than Silver

Lord, You are more precious than silver,
Lord, You are more costly than gold,
Lord, You are more beautiful than diamonds,
And nothing I desire compares with You.

And who can weigh the value of knowing You?
Who can judge the worth of who You are?
Who can count the blessings of loving You?
Who can say just how great You are?

CHAPTER TWO

PRAISE HIM

Therefore we praise you, joining our voices with
Angels and Archangels and
with all the company of heaven, who for ever sing this hymn
to proclaim the glory of your Name.[2]

One worship song among all I've written seems to be the enduring favorite with the members of Liberty Church, my spiritual
home in Birmingham. It is called "Praise Him"—simple enough—and
we come back to it time and again in our worship services. I especially
love to lead it during Holy Communion because that's where the song
always takes us—into the presence of the Lord and that life-giving
communion with our heavenly Father.

"Praise Him" is one of my early efforts, written in 1984 while I
was living in Ann Arbor, Michigan, and part of the worship ministry
of Cornerstone Christian Church. I went on a ten-day, liquids-only
fast that winter for the purposes of seeking the Lord and praying for
guidance in several areas. I have kept a journal only sporadically over
the years, so I don't have a written record of my devotional life from
every period. But at that time in my life, I wrote in my journal a lot,
and I still have my notes from that particular fast.

My entries from that time are a mixture of my thoughts on paper,
my questions to the Lord, and the many prayers I recorded. I made
notes about how I felt from day to day and what kinds of liquids I was

drinking and when. Although I know "Praise Him" was begun during that time, the only written remarks I have about it are "Worked on a few song ideas."

But if memory serves me, this is how it happened: late into the fast I ventured out on a Saturday for a morning run around the apartment complex where I live. I was long past the initial bodily discomfort that fasting brings and felt completely energized as I ran under a cloudless, bright blue sky and gulped in the crisp air. As I prayed and fellow-shipped with the Lord, I soon heard what sounded like an anointed, melodic download from heaven. I heard within my spirit angelic voices singing this beautiful chorus: "Praise Him!" It contained more notes than seemed possible for just two one-syllable words.

I finished my run, returned to my townhouse, grabbed my guitar and a tape recorder, and sang into it my best rendition of what I had just heard. In the days following, I added two verses to the chorus. Soon my church began singing "Praise Him" during our worship services.

At the time of the fast, I was also working on a small-budget re-cording of some of the praise and worship songs I had written. When "Praise Him" was finished, it was added to the list. The project was produced by John Conner. John was a friend who at that time was the worship leader of our church. John had just begun to explore his grow-ing interest in the recording arts and had purchased some equipment. While John had a little experience with recording music, I had none. So we recorded my first-ever project on his newly acquired Fostex 8-track tape recorder, which was set up in the storefront space where our church met. (For all you gearheads, this was a reel-to-reel analog machine that used quarter-inch tape.)

If you told me today that you own a copy, I'd sneak in your house to get that tape back! It's not an impressive recording at all. But in retrospect, I can see that God's hand was definitely on this early col-laboration and on our separate pursuits.

Twenty-five years later, I'm still writing songs. John now owns a music production studio in Brentwood, Tennessee, where he continues to serve both his clients and the kingdom of God with his many gifts.

After the master recording was completed, I had cassette copies, titled "More Precious Than Silver," made at a Detroit-area duplicating business. I remember that duplicator well because I was once given a carton of *The Temptations—Greatest Hits* by mistake when I picked up an order. I returned the carton, although I'm sure I could have sold their cassettes more easily than mine! I then made the cassettes available to our church right away; the members had generously funded my production expenses through financial gifts and prepurchases. I also compiled a small mailing list of churches around the United States and mailed out cassettes as gifts. As rudimentary as this recording was, it seemed important to share what we had done with other like-minded churches who might appreciate the songs.

Praise and worship recordings were still something of a rare commodity by the mid-1980s, which might be hard for some of you to believe, considering what is available today. But interest in such music was growing exponentially across the body of Christ as God poured out a renewal of true worship upon the church. In response to the hunger in God's people to experience His presence in praise and worship, quality "live" recordings soon began to be produced by visionary companies, such as Integrity Music.

"Praise Him" was eventually recorded by Integrity Music, although it took a few more years and a more-polished recording of it to convince anyone that the mildly challenging chorus could actually be sung by a congregation.

In 1985 I was contacted by John Sellers, a fellow worship songwriter I knew through Maranatha Campus Ministries. John called to say he was interested in producing an album for me. He had recently completed a recording of his songs with the help of Buck and Annie Herring of the musical group 2nd Chapter of Acts and was still excited about that whole creative process as well as his time with them. His project was called *Let Praise Arise*. It was the first worship recording ever distributed to the direct-mail subscribers of the ministry that would soon become Integrity's Hosanna! Music (known today as Integrity Music, a division of Integrity Media).

When John contacted me, he was eager to get back into a recording studio. For my part, by then I had two small-budget recordings under my belt. I was hungry to do more, and I was excited anyone would take this kind of interest in my music, whatever his motivation.

The prospect of working out of a "real" recording studio was also thrilling.

We soon started working together on a recording of my songs, titled *More Precious Than Silver—Songs of Celebration and Worship*. All the tracks except the background vocals were recorded at a studio in Pasadena, Texas, because John lived in that area at the time. The background vocals were done in Muscle Shoals, Alabama. John contracted this work with Lenny LeBlanc, who put together a wonderful group of singers. In addition to him, there was Will McFarlane, Paul Baloche, Kelly Willard, Rita Gannon (soon to be Baloche), and Cindy Richardson. If you know anything about the world of Christian music, you will recognize that these were—and are—some of the best vocalists, musicians, and writers on the planet. It's amazing to me that they were willing to sing on my project back then. Most of my songs at the time were nowhere near being in their league! Still, several gems came out of this recording. One of the best cuts was "Praise Him," which had this wonderful, anointed group vocal on the chorus performed by Kelly, Rita, and Cindy. What amazing voices!

My 1986 recording of "Praise Him" became the prototype for the beautiful arrangement Integrity Music recorded in 1993 with worship leader Bob Fitts. Little did I know that both Kelly and Rita would also sing "Praise Him" for Bob's project, *Proclaim His Power*. I was actually in the audience the night it was recorded "live" at Christ Church in Nashville. It was genuinely a special moment in the evening for me as the congregation sang "Praise Him" in worship with Kelly and Rita singing the verses, each in her unique way. The anointing on the song that was present when I first heard the heavenly version was very much evident that night, too.

And so it seems to remain.

One of my favorite stories connected to this song—which I learned only a couple of years ago—has to do with the way two of my professional peers reacted the first time they saw the chorus lyrics projected on a screen. I am totally sympathetic to how underwhelmed they must have been at the time; "Praise Him, praise Him, praise Him, praise Him" is hardly the stuff of great lyric writing!

"But then," as one man was humble enough to tell me, "we began to sing it, and all I could do was weep!"

I grin every time I think about that!

Praise Him

We have assembled to praise the One we love,
We join the chorus of angels up above,
Who sing hosannas and their praises to our King,
We join our voices together and we sing,

Praise Him, praise Him!
Praise Him, praise Him!

We are Your children, we've come to seek Your face,
We have come boldly before the throne of grace,
To love and worship You and listen to Your voice,
You are our Father and how our hearts rejoice.

Praise Him, praise Him!
Praise Him, praise Him!

CHAPTER THREE

LEAD ME TO
THE ROCK

Hear my cry, O God; give heed to my prayer.
From the end of the earth I call to You when my heart is faint;
Lead me to the rock that is higher than I.
—Psalm 61:1–2

Years ago it was not uncommon for people who had just heard one of my songs to comment, "Wow, you must have really been through some tough things!"

Or something like that.

I'd smile politely but always wonder what in the world they were talking about. After all, I'd grown up in a normal, churchgoing, American family, unmarred by the tragedy we tend to associate with dysfunction. So why the comments?

Here's what I've learned: "normal" is just a setting on the dryer. The truth is, everyone has lived through some kind of difficulty just by virtue of having been born into this fallen and sinful world. We've all hit rough patches along the way, and I'm no exception. In fact, coming into wholeness in certain areas has been a lifelong struggle for me.

I'd have to say that my life has been a blessed one overall. Still, "normal" in my life means I can't remember a day when I was truly happy about being a girl until after my college years. I had a deep sense of being rejected because of my gender. While as a child I could not have articulated my feelings about this, my feelings profoundly shaped my behavior and my emotional development well into adulthood. "Normal" also meant I had frequent, debilitating migraines from age five all the way through high school. The headaches caused me to miss a lot of school days, and I spent a lot of time making up missed assignments. I was thankful to have been a good student and able to keep up with my work. I carried medication with me at all times so I could take something before the migraine got so bad that I had to leave school. Even with that precaution, my mother—God bless her—still made a lot of trips to pick me up because I was too miserable to finish my classes. If my headache became full-blown, my only option was to lie down in a noiseless, dark room, sometimes for several days. This was a very isolating experience for me, and it contributed to the rejection I felt deep inside. The headaches finally stopped, which is a story all its own. I honestly don't think I could have made it through college if God had not begun to heal me when He did.

Today, I suspect the migraines were caused by the great deal of suppressed anger over the rejection I felt as a young child. The root of the rage, however, would not be uncovered and healed until I was almost fifty years old.

Many wonderful things about my childhood I am deeply grateful for. I was blessed with loving parents and a stable home. I had plenty of friends and enjoyed the many advantages a middle-class upbringing afforded. I wouldn't trade my family for anyone else's, in spite of that terrible sense of inferiority and rejection, which I believe were connected to some of my earliest moments of life. I have no memory of them, of course, and I still don't completely understand all of it. But I do have some insight from the Lord about how these things came to be, which are beyond the scope of this book to delve into. I can tell you, however, that the pain of my early wounds drove me in ways that neither I nor my parents understood.

From early on I hated being a girl, so I instinctively modeled my behavior and mannerisms after my father. Understanding the myriad of difficulties my tomboyish mannerisms could create for me later in life, my mother valiantly tried to correct me. This led to no end of conflicts between us.

"We thought it was cute when you walked like your father at age four," she said. "It's not cute anymore!"

One of the biggest fights we ever had was over her decision to enrolled me in a "charm and modeling" school during my sophomore year of high school. I attended with heels dragging all the way. If that wasn't the worst year of my life, it was easily in the top five.

Conflict added to conflict. As a Christian, I knew I needed to obey my mother, but I simply wasn't secure enough in my true identify as a young woman to embrace the instruction of the school. Truth was, I was terrified. When you're inwardly conflicted about yourself, no amount of enforced behavior modification will change you. Not for long anyway.

I also developed an unconscious pattern of rejecting people before they could reject me. I'm sure this was an attempt to protect myself from pain, but in the end it only caused a lot more of it for me.

Interestingly, the one song from my youth I can still remember all the words to is Paul Simon's "I Am a Rock," which I think is quite telling. I believe I was drawn to the song because it gave voice to something I felt deeply but could neither identify nor express. I identified with its plaintive words describing a rock as feeling no pain and with its last line that reminds listeners that islands never cry.

Somewhere along the way I determined that pain of any kind was a bad thing and should be avoided at all costs. As I did with my migraines, I did everything possible to manage emotional pain in the early stages before it began roaring at full volume and laid me out. As I grew older, this unhealthy tendency caused me to shut down emotionally. I don't mean that I was ever mentally unstable or unable to function in daily life. I actually developed a very dry wit and a sharp sense of comedic timing, which I'm sure was, at least in part, a coping mechanism. I was, however, growing vaguely aware that something inside really hurt. I couldn't name it, but that didn't matter because I really didn't want to deal with it. Instead, for many years I remained completely out of touch with the pain on a rational level.

If you've ever tried to hold a beach ball underwater, you know that the task takes constant effort. The ball will come bursting up to the surface if you let go of it for even an instant. I finally got to the point where I could not hold down the ball any longer, and my pain started popping up to the surface.

While in my childhood I suffered from migraines, by the time I was in my forties, the suppressed rage began manifesting itself in my body as a mild form of fibromyalgia. If anything ever banged up against the still-open wounds of my rejection issues, I'd either "go off" about something as a hint of the rage erupted or retreat deeper into my self-protective mode.

It was rare for me to lose my temper though. I'd usually just withdraw and keep my emotions at bay. I eventually sought the help of spiritual counselors and friends, who helped me trace the visible fruit back to the invisible root of my anger. They listened to the Holy Spirit with me as He began to shine light into my darkness. They prayed with the authority of Jesus into the hurt places, and I began to heal. None of this process has been instant or easy, but the healing has been both ongoing and profound.

An old saying says, "Time heals all wounds." It is true that healing is a process that takes place with time, but time itself heals nothing. If anything, the passage of time only allows an unattended injury or offense to grow much worse and create more damage. It is only the forgiveness of sins through Jesus Christ that heals us. All the wounds and sins of our past have to be brought to His cross, no matter how long ago they occurred or how slight they may seem to us now. Our sins must be confessed to God and to one another and be repented of.

Because we were wounded in specific ways, we must learn to forgive in specific ways and to receive God's forgiveness in order for healing to occur. This is true even for injuries to the soul that happened so early in life that we have no visual memory of them (the memory may be in our emotions or in our body as opposed to a picture we can recall). And we must rely on the Holy Spirit to reveal them, of course, when that is what is needed.

In those days, I loved Jesus from childhood and was trying to follow Him with all my heart. I belonged to the Lord, but I was a mess! For nearly my whole life I had been angry to the point of rage and didn't know it. I desperately needed to find both expression and healing for my pain. But God knew all about my issues, and He who gives songs in the night began to sing to me.

I do believe that my becoming a songwriter and a worship leader saved my life. God kept me in life until I could get to the place where I could receive the deep level of healing I needed so badly. It eventually came through the ministry of skilled and compassionate prayer ministers empowered by the Holy Spirit and through the love of His people in my life. Coming into wholeness is not a do-it-yourself project, as it turns out.

I was so out of touch with my deep heart when I began writing that only years later I realized how many of my songs were written not just *through* me but *for* me. I needed great healing, so they carried great healing. I believe they still do. "Lead Me to the Rock," based on Psalm 61, is one of those songs.

I don't remember much about the writing of this song except sitting on the bed with my guitar and my Bible open to the book of Psalms. The Lord knew what I needed long before I did, and the age-old cry of the psalmist also became my cry. Maybe that's why the song has always been one of my favorites.

Recently, I met a young woman named Heather at a residential Christian ministry to women. She was there, along with several others like her, working through the fallout of a painful past and a lifestyle of wrong choices. After I ministered to the ladies in song, I joined them for lunch. Heather, who sat beside me, told me how meaningful "Lead Me to the Rock" had become to her when, at eight years old, she suffered through the tumult of her parents' divorce. Her eyes glistened with tears as she said, "I felt like that song was written just for me!"

Her story touched me deeply. And I pray that you, too, will find this song to be as great a comfort to the painful places of your life as it has been to both Heather's and to mine.

Lead Me to the Rock

When my heart is overwhelmed, hear my cry,
Give heed to my prayer.
When my eyes are dim with tears,
Oh Father, make them clear.
From the ends of all the earth, when my heart is fainting,
Let me know that You have heard.
Lead me into safety.

And lead me to the Rock, the Rock that's higher.
Lead me to the Rock that's higher than I.
Lead me to the Rock, the Rock that's higher,
Higher than I.

You, O Lord, have been for me a refuge from my enemy.
Let me live within Your strength,
In the shelter of Your wings.
From the ends of all the earth, when my heart is fainting,
Let me know that You have heard.
Lead me into safety.

And lead me to the Rock, the Rock that's higher.
Lead me to the Rock that's higher than I.
Lead me to the Rock, the Rock that's higher,
Higher than I.

CHAPTER FOUR

TURN MY HEART

The king's heart is like channels of water in the hand of the Lord;
He turns it wherever He wishes.
—Proverbs 21:1

I've always been drawn to American folk melodies, especially the early
ones handed down from the English and Celtic peoples who settled
this country. I remember learning the sailor's chantey "Shenandoah" as
an elementary school child and thinking how wonderful that melody
was. Especially the part that goes, "Awaaaay, you rolling river!"

I was hooked from that time on.

I'm a descendant of northern Europeans primarily. My mother was
a Key and her mother a Pierce; I'm pretty sure both names hail from
the British Isles. My father is of French ancestry. "DeShazo" is the
phonetic spelling of "de Chazeaux" or perhaps "de Chezeaux." A vil-
lage still bears the name somewhere just over the French border near
Lausanne, Switzerland. In addition, there are family links to the Scots
and the Welsh. I suspect all that Celtic DNA came right on through
to me. I'm sure that's why I've always loved hymns like "Come Thou
Fount of Every Blessing" and "When I Survey the Wondrous Cross,"
as set to the Irish tune "Slane." Both hymns are usually designated in
modern hymnals as having traditional American or Appalachian folk
melodies. They have great lyrics, of course, but it's their melodies that
first made me fall in love with them.

I've lived in Alabama nearly all of my life and mostly in the Birmingham area. Other than there, I moved to Ann Arbor, Michigan, in the fall of 1981 with a church-planting team. I lived there for eight years. When I informed my parents of my plans to go with a campus ministry to southeastern Michigan and find a job, my dad's incredulous reaction was "Nobody moves *to* Michigan to get a job!"

It was true. Michigan's economy was floundering in the wake of spiking global energy and gasoline prices, which took a heavy toll on its auto industry (Michigan is home to Ford, GM, and Chrysler) and on the manufacturing sector. Workers in need of jobs were leaving the state in droves so much so that the popular saying was "Last one to leave Michigan, turn out the lights!" It wasn't easy, but I eventually found employment in an information systems department within the medical school of the University of Michigan, Ann Arbor's biggest employer.

Michigan is a beautiful state. I especially loved it in the fall, when the air turned crisp and the hardwood trees seemed to burst into brilliant color. I never failed to marvel, while standing on the shore of Lake Michigan or Lake Superior, that the wide expanse of water I was looking at was actually a body of fresh water and not an ocean. But Michigan never quite felt like home to me, and I'm not a big fan of extremely cold winters, major snowfalls, or Big 10 football. So after nearly two years of restless thinking, I made plans to move south again in the early fall of 1989. I was excited to be going but saddened too at the prospect of leaving good friends and the local church I had helped to plant and lead worship for. Saying good-bye was a lot tougher than I had imagined it would be.

I had only needed a few square feet of a shared moving van to get my belongings to Ann Arbor. I hadn't even owned a car yet, so I helped drive someone else's for the eight hundred-plus mile trip from Auburn, Alabama. When I packed up and left eight years later, I needed a seventeen-foot U-Haul truck with a towing package for my red Sentra station wagon. Friends from the church helped me move boxes out of my second-floor apartment and into the back of the truck. They were a great help in getting the load secured for the move; I just wished they had noticed those "this end up" arrows on the wardrobe boxes!

One of the young men—a friend of mine from the church—met me early the next morning to help drive the truck down, and I put him on a plane back to Michigan the next day. I waved good-bye, and a significant chapter of my life came to an end. I will always be grateful for the lessons I learned while living in Michigan, the ministry opportunities I had there, and the friends I made. I was stretched a lot during those years, and my faith in God grew as a result.

When I returned to Birmingham, I had temporarily moved in with my parents, and I was less than six months into the first year of my songwriter's contract with Integrity Music. I had a small monthly income in the form of an advance against my royalty earnings with the potential for more. But I never wanted to sit in a room and write songs eight hours a day, so I soon found a part-time job in a packaging and shipping store just to get myself out of the house. I did write a lot though, especially during the first few months I was home. When I wasn't working at Mail Boxes Etc., I was often down in my parents' finished basement, sitting at the desk I had set up in one corner of the den to work on my song ideas.

Even though I had returned to a place familiar to me, in many respects I was starting over. I needed to find somewhere to live, a new church, and new friends; and I had a lot of questions about my future. I had known my place in the world while I was a part of the church in Michigan, but where was it now? Could I find a church that would give me an outlet for the worship songs I was writing? Could I make a go of it as a songwriter? I sure didn't want to make a career out of Mail Boxes Etc. (now known as The UPS Store), but what did God desire for me, and how could I find that road?

On an October morning in 1989, I came to Proverbs 21 in my daily Scripture reading. The chapter begins, "The king's heart is like channels of water in the hand of the Lord; He turns it wherever He wishes."

I remember praying, "I don't know about the king, Lord, but I do know that I need You to turn my heart like channels of water."

So I began to sing that verse as I worshipped, changing the wording to reflect my deeply felt prayer.

Turn my heart, O Lord, like channels of water

No, not channels, I thought. *What about rivers?* I tried again.

Turn my heart, O Lord, like rivers of water,
Turn my heart, O Lord, by Your hand,

Much better! I sang on, giving voice to the cry of my heart and instinctively choosing a melody characteristic of my ancestral roots.

'Til my whole life flows in the river of Your Spirit,
And my name brings honor to the Lamb.

I wanted God to guide me and to help me live my life in a way that would bring glory to Him. Those few lines said it as well as I knew how to say it. A few days later, I finished up the song that I titled "Turn My Heart" and sang it often during my personal times with the Lord in this season of new beginnings.

God is faithful. He helped me find everything I was looking for as I started to build a new life for myself in Birmingham. I found a place to live and a spiritual family to call "home"; they welcomed me and my songs. In time He answered a lot of my questions, not by telling me everything in advance but by requiring me to walk with Him by faith, one day at a time. As I simply asked for His guidance in prayer, He gave it. The Lord still insists on this arrangement! So twenty years from the day I wrote it, "Turn My Heart" is still a song that deeply resounds with me and is still my prayer.

Turn My Heart

Turn my heart, O Lord, like rivers of water,
Turn my heart, O Lord, by Your hand,
'Til my whole life flows in the river of Your Spirit,
And my name brings honor to the Lamb.

Lord, I surrender to Your work in me.
I rest my life within Your loving hands.

TURN MY HEART

Turn my heart, O Lord, like rivers of water,
Turn my heart, O Lord, by Your hand,
'Til my whole life flows in the river of Your Spirit,
And my name brings honor to the Lamb.

CHAPTER FIVE

BE MAGNIFIED

Therefore, since the children share in flesh and blood, He Himself likewise also partook of the same, that through death He might render powerless him who had the power of death, that is, the devil, and might free those who through the fear of death were subject to slavery all their lives.
—Hebrews 2:14–15

Perhaps you're familiar with the old adage "What you don't know can't hurt you." In my opinion nothing could be further from the truth. My own mother could have died because of my inability to act in the face of my irrational fear.

In recent years I was surprised to learn that I nearly choked to death shortly after my birth. My mother is a little foggy about the details, but according to her account, I had to have my airway cleared after I'd been taken from the delivery room to the nursery. For many years I had no knowledge of this incident, but when I learned of it, it explained a curious phenomenon that happened to me throughout childhood and into my thirties.

Sometimes just as I was about to drift into a deep sleep, I was overtaken by a terrible sense of fear and panic. I then struggled to try to move a foot or to shake my head until I was fully awake. Rationally, I knew I was only falling asleep, but something irrational in me was terrified. Somehow the awareness that I was about to lose consciousness triggered the memory of my near-death experience on the day I was born. My body's memory told me that if I lost consciousness I could die, so I fought desperately to wake myself up.

A confirming incident happened to me around age eleven. One night I heard my mother go into the bathroom across the hall from my bedroom. She was choking so hard that the blood in her face came up to the surface of her pores. I could hear her struggling, but I couldn't move to get out of bed and go to her aid. I think my experience of nearly choking to death as a newborn was the reason for my paralyzing fear. The terror of that moment remained trapped in my body and rendered me helpless in my own mother's distress that night. Thank God, she recovered her breath because no one in the family got up to help her.

It's one thing to be afraid of something you can't recall and quite another when you remember what happened to you. Twice I was attacked by a dog while taking a walk in my neighborhood. The first time, I was bitten in the calf by a territorial mutt who had escaped his owner's backyard fence. The second time, I was knocked to the ground by a wild-eyed, sixty-five-pound boxer, who inexplicably leapt out of a pickup truck's cab and ran straight for me. Both times were traumatic, and I suffered very impressive bruises and abrasions. I've been apprehensive about walking in my own neighborhood ever since. I do it, but it frightens me to see an unfamiliar dog roaming about. The fear tied to the memory of these attacks tells me they could happen again. I might have given up walking outside altogether because of my fear. But knowing what I was dealing with helped me to move toward overcoming my fear of another attack.

What if, however, you have no picture of an event to match the overwhelming emotion of your fear (or anger or sadness or anxiety)? How do you even know that you need help, much less to begin to ask for it? And if an identifiable fear can cripple you in certain areas of life, what could an unknown one do?

The mother of all fear is the fear of death. We're not really afraid of the dark, for example. We're afraid of what might happen to us in the dark, namely death. If you are always afraid of dying, however subconsciously that fear resides, what hope do you have of living a truly free and robust life? Not much, I'd say, for along with fear comes a host of other things, such as hopelessness, difficulty in taking risks, unbelief, and even despair.

Somewhere deep within, we may question, as did Eve in the garden, whether God is really good. We come to believe Satan's lies about God as well as his lies about us. Thirty-plus years was a long time to carry the subconscious memory of nearly dying. Occasionally I'll get a flash of insight about how this, compounded with other issues, has affected me. Only God knows the full extent of it. Only God knew what it would take to deliver me from the snare of lies believed, however unwittingly I came to believe them. Once again, the first overtures of healing came to me on the wings of a song.

One morning during the closing weeks of 1990, I sat down at my desk to listen through some song ideas I had previously recorded on tape and in hopes of finding something that showed enough promise to become a song. Instead, I picked up my guitar, strummed a chord, and was quite startled to hear something similar to these words come out of my mouth:

> I have made You too small in my eyes, O Lord, forgive me
> And I have believed in a lie, that You were unable to help me

I just sat there in stunned silence for several minutes. I had no idea where I might have come up with such a thought, but I distinctly remember saying to myself out loud, "I think that's important!"

I recorded my melody and lyric idea for the song on a cassette tape and set it aside for further development. Over the next few weeks, I pondered those initial lyrics and asked the Lord's help for the direction the song should take.

I finished writing "Be Magnified" in early January 1991. A sense of quiet satisfaction filled my heart when I knew the song was completed. I had a confidence in my spirit that this song was significant. I didn't know in what way, of course. I just knew it intuitively.

I began teaching "Be Magnified" at my church and other places where I had occasion to lead worship or to share a new song. In every place I sang it, the song seemed to evoke a strong response in God's people as they worshipped. Then my hopes for the song were realized as word got back to me that churches I'd never set foot in were singing it in their worship services, too. In 1993, Integrity Music selected "Be Magnified" for a live Hosanna! Music worship project that was to be recorded in Jacksonville, Florida, featuring worship leader Randy Rothwell. Some in attendance that evening said that the singing of "Be Magnified" was a very powerful moment in the context of that night's worship. In fact, the recording itself would be released with the title "Be Magnified."

I was astounded at the initial response to the song. It seemed to strike such a deep place in the hearts of people whenever they sang it. Pastors have shared with me how their entire church was deeply touched by the Lord through this song. Friends from Michigan told me that the song was used a great deal during ministry time for pastors and leaders at the Toronto Airport Church during the early days of the Toronto Blessing. Several people have taken the time to write to me with their individual testimonies concerning the encouragement "Be Magnified" has been to them. The song even played an important role in Evander Holyfield's upset win over Mike Tyson to become World Heavyweight Champion.

In that upset, Evander become the second man in boxing to become World Heavyweight Champion for the third time. He later admitted to struggling during training camp with his rhythm and timing. Discouraged and already a twenty-five-to-one underdog, he called his wife early one morning. She encouraged him, then sang "Be Magnified" to him and persuaded him to sing along with her. That call was Evander's turning point.

In the February 1997 issue of *Ebony* magazine and in her article "The Lady and the Champ," Laura B. Randolph quotes Evander. "Once I started singing that song, my speed, my rhythm, my timing started coming back to me. I sang that song so much; everybody in my camp knew it."[3]

In the moments before he came out to face Tyson, Holyfield had his entire camp sing "Be Magnified" with him in the locker room. The fight was over with less than a minute left in the eleventh round. Giving glory to God, Evander Holyfield won a tremendous victory in one of the biggest upsets in boxing history.

I am awed when I hear such reports, and I am reminded afresh that we all struggle with basically the same things in this life.

And that we all need Jesus.

I must admit that when I first wrote "Be Magnified," I did not recognize that God was trying to get through to me about the condition of my own soul. My mindset about songwriting was so geared toward using my gifts to serve the body of Christ that it never occurred to me that perhaps the message was meant for me. I simply did not hear the cry of my own spirit. The need for confession and repentance was mine. The cry for deliverance was mine. The song of praise was mine, too.

God is so merciful. While He patiently waited for the power of the words that first poured out of my own mouth to break upon my heart and minister to my own need, He blessed millions more with "Be Magnified."

Hallelujah!

Be Magnified

I have made You too small in my eyes,
O Lord, forgive me.
And I have believed in a lie,
That You were unable to help me.
But now, O Lord, I see my wrong.
Heal my heart and show Yourself strong.
And in my eyes and with my song,
O Lord, be magnified.
O Lord, be magnified.

Be magnified, O Lord!
You are highly exalted.
And there is nothing You can't do.
O Lord, my eyes are on You.
Be magnified!
O Lord, be magnified!

I have leaned on the wisdom of men,
O God, forgive me.
And I have responded to them,

Instead of Your light and Your mercy.
But now, O Lord, I see my wrong.
Heal my heart and show Yourself strong.
And in my eyes and with my song,
O Lord, be magnified.
O Lord, be magnified.

Be magnified, O Lord!
You are highly exalted.
And there is nothing You can't do.
O Lord, my eyes are on You.
Be magnified!
O Lord, be magnified!

Words and music by Lynn DeShazo
©1992 Integrity's Hosanna! Music/ASCAP

CHAPTER SIX

IN YOUR PRESENCE, O GOD

He who dwells in the shelter of the Most High will abide
in the shadow of the Almighty.
—Psalm 91:1

Those curious about the creative process often ask me how I go about writing songs. "Do they just come to you?" is the one question I hear most frequently.

No short answer could satisfy either me or the person posing the question, but I can honestly say that "In Your Presence, O God" is, indeed, a song that just "came to me." I did not sit down one day to write this song out of a personal experience or a clever idea. It began to flow to me from the Holy Spirit during the autumn of 1993, and I simply paid attention.

One day, as I recall, I was going about my daily activities when this line began to play through my head:

> I want to go where the rivers cannot overflow me,
> Where my feet are on a rock

The idea came quietly but with great persistence. I spent several weeks just living with and working on this song, mostly because it wouldn't go away! I completed it in late December and eventually taught it to my local church on a Sunday morning. It was well received by the congregation, and a powerful anointing began to flow as we worshipped the Lord with it.

What struck me about the initial lyric idea was the meaning of the word *rivers*. I wrote this song right before several notable revivals broke out around the world, and many people were wonderfully touched by the Holy Spirit in an outpouring that came to be referred to as "the river of God." A number of songs with that theme were written and spread rapidly among churches experiencing this move of God. The rivers my song referred to, however, were not the life-giving waters of God's Spirit described in Ezekiel 47. These were the rivers of Isaiah 43:2. I had a sense that this song was being given to encourage God's people in times of great difficulty.

Soon, however, I found myself questioning whether I had misinterpreted the theme of "rivers" as I'd believed it to be when the song idea first came to me. After all, believers around the globe were experiencing renewal and refreshment. Everyone was splashing around in "the river of God." It was wonderful! It was marvelous! River songs were "in"!

But what I had written was about wanting to be in a place where the water—rivers of adversity and a flood of evil—can't overwhelm you. I felt out of sync with what God was doing in that particular season. In fact, I have often struggled with the tension created in me by writing songs like this one. I'll have an inner knowing about the significance of a song yet still be frustrated by the timing of its release.

Prophetic songs tend to be slightly ahead of the current spiritual season when they first emerge. A song like "In Your Presence, O God" is prophetic in nature; it ministers in the present moment, but it also speaks of things yet to come. No wonder I felt out of sync because, in a way, I was. My first impression about the "rivers" was right on though. The horrible events of September 11, 2001, in which over three thousand American lives were lost in a terrorist attack on our own soil, may be a foreshadowing of the kinds of difficulties that many will face in the days that are upon us. But followers of Jesus can take great comfort in knowing that our Lord has promised never to leave us or forsake us. Consider these words from the prophet Isaiah:

But now, thus says the Lord, your Creator, O Jacob,
And He who formed you, O Israel, "Do not fear, for I have

redeemed you; I have called you by name; you are Mine!
When you pass through the waters, I will be with you;
And through the rivers, they will not overflow you.
When you walk through the fire, you will not be scorched,
Nor will the flame burn you."

—Isaiah 43:1–2

Our faithful God will not only lead us through our fiery trials but also be there with us in the midst of them.

Paul Wilbur, a Jewish believer in Jesus and an anointed worship leader, was the first to record "In Your Presence, O God." He recorded it "live" in Jerusalem for an Integrity Music project called *Shalom Jerusalem*. I think it's significant that the Scripture from Isaiah that inspired this song addresses Israel so specifically. It was, after all, first spoken by the prophet to comfort the Jewish people. And I have always loved that the song was released to the world from Jerusalem, the city where King David first inaugurated continual praise and worship before the ark of the Lord.

I met Paul for the first time eight years after this popular recording was released in 1995. He graciously thanked me for the song and then told me that a recurring testimony he received concerning its ministry came from women who struggled with infertility. He also told me recently that he heard three testimonies from women who reported how deeply the song had ministered to them in the midst of great personal tragedy—having to bury their infants. He added, "I'll wager that song has been sung at more funerals than you know."

That's amazing to me! It reminds me, too, that whether our trouble is headlining the news or concerns our personal pain, we can find strength to endure the onslaughts that threaten to overwhelm us and the courage to overcome in the refuge of His presence.

Paul recently shared with me that "In Your Presence, O God" is a song he still consistently uses in his ministry "probably," he said, "75 percent of the time."

It's always rewarding to have one of my songs recorded by an artist of Paul's caliber. But it's even more gratifying for me to know that a song has a life of its own, well beyond a recording—in the hearts of God's people who need His comforting, strengthening presence.

In Your Presence, O God

I want to go where the rivers cannot overflow me,
Where my feet are on a rock.
I want to hide where the blazing fire cannot burn me,
In Your Presence, O God.

In Your Presence, that's where I am strong,
In Your Presence, O Lord my God.
In Your Presence, that's where I belong,
Seeking Your face, touching Your grace,
In the cleft of the rock,
In Your Presence, O God.

I want to hide where the flood of evil cannot reach me,
Where I'm covered by Your blood.
I want to be where the schemes of darkness
cannot touch me,
In Your presence, O God.

In Your Presence, that's where I am strong,
In Your Presence, O Lord my God.
In Your Presence, that's where I belong,
Seeking Your face, touching Your grace,
In the cleft of the rock,
In Your Presence, O God.

You are my firm foundation, I trust in You all day long.
I am Your child and Your servant.
And You are my strength and my song.
You're my song.

CHAPTER SEVEN

BE UNTO YOUR NAME

And they sang a new song, saying,
"Worthy are You to take the book and to break its seals;
for You were slain, and purchased for God
with Your blood men from every tribe and
tongue and people and nation."
—Revelation 5:9

In a songwriter's world, two heads are often better than one. In December 1996, I drove from my home in Birmingham, Alabama, to Franklin, Tennessee, for a cowriting session with my friend Gary Sadler. It wasn't a great time to be on the road actually. North Alabama was covered in a layer of ice from our occasional winter storms, and Interstate 65 north of Cullman was down to one lane in places. I white-knuckled it to the state line, where the roads suddenly became completely free of snow and ice.

Mystified by the contrast but greatly relieved, I drove the last hour without incident and arrived safely at the Sadler home. After a bit of catching-up conversation and something to eat, we spent that afternoon and the next morning working on various song ideas. I remember starting the verse lyric for "Be Unto Your Name" at the kitchen table during a lunch break. Between bites of food I blurted out, "We are a moment, You are forever."

I really don't remember the line of conversation that prompted me, but that's how the song began. We took that beginning and started to write again after lunch.

Gary has a better memory of the day, thankfully. He says, "We started talking about how fragile and temporal—just a vapor, a moment—life is, how our lives pass so quickly, and yet God's life goes on forever."

What I do remember is that we started the song easily enough, but writing the rest of it soon became a challenge. Gary and I stumbled around for what felt like an hour, but we were getting nowhere. We finally just stopped what we were doing and asked the Lord to help us. There soon followed a moment, as the song came together at last, that a portal of heaven seemed to open up to us as we worshipped and sang the chorus.

> Holy, holy, Lord God Almighty
> Worthy is the Lamb Who was slain
> Highest praises, honor and glory
> Be unto Your name, be unto Your name

Here are Gary's words again:

"We both instantly loved the song, I think mainly because we knew we had tapped into something that had been lying deep within our hearts, and also because it seemed to echo the heart expression of every believer—awe, humility, and reverence in the light of One so great."

We recorded a demo of the song that day, and Gary later sent a copy to Integrity Music, our publisher at the time. Mission accomplished, right? Not quite.

Finishing a song and submitting it for publication is only part of the battle to see a song released for ministry. I have therefore learned to pay attention to impressions the Lord gives me about particular songs. "Be Unto Your Name" became one of those songs for me. I carried it in my spirit, often praying that God would release it in His time. The first time I heard the song as recorded on the popular Integrity's Hosanna! Music project, *Revival in Belfast*, I spontaneously burst into tears of joy. What an answer to prayer!

Some of the most meaningful words to me in "Be Unto Your Name" are found in the second verse.

We are the broken, You are the healer
Jesus, Redeemer, mighty to save

I have a long history with Jesus. I can never remember a time when I did not know about Him or believe in Him. I responded with my heart to the good news of John 3:16 around age eleven, and I trusted Him as my Savior, as much as I understood what I was doing at the time. As I grew older, I also managed to avoid all the obvious "thou shall nots" most of my generation considered to be significant, such as murder, starting a riot, or using illegal substances. Oh, I agreed with all the Scriptures like Romans 3:23 (For all have sinned and fall short of the glory of God), which meant that I, too, was a sinner. Who's dumb enough to argue with God about the matter? But it's only been in recent years that I've come to understand how great a capacity I have for sin or, consequently, how much woundedness was in my own soul. I have to tell you that as disturbing as it was to discover such things about myself, it is both a blessing and the mercy of God. I simply could not come to repentance and healing for my sinful and broken condition as long as I was blind to it.

About twice a year I have the privilege of leading worship for a healing prayer conference conducted by my friends Clay and Mary McLean. One of the things they always make clear in every conference is the necessity of forgiving others and of receiving God's forgiveness for ourselves to experience true and lasting healing.

As I have heard them say so many times, "Whatever you do not forgive, you will either become or you will transfer to others." Transference—in case you are unfamiliar with this psychological phenomenon—has to do with reacting to a person in your present because of something that happened in your past that is still unresolved. When the Holy Spirit began to show me the people I needed to forgive in relation to past hurts, I began to realize how much transference I have done throughout my life. I am sorry to say that there is an impressive debris trail of persons in my wake who, unfortunately for them, physically resembled in some way the individuals who had hurt me. This was usually a family member because those we are closest to relationally are often the ones who hurt us most deeply. Of course, we are often guilty of hurting them, too.

Let me give you a couple of examples of how the sinful response of transference worked in my life to hurt both me and others.

My father is an emotionally reserved and stoic man. He's really just an old softie, but you'd never know it because he looks so serious most of the time. When he yelled at me as a child (which was rare), the event was like an ambush—completely surprising. I remember being in the basement with him one Saturday while he worked on one of his perpetual home maintenance projects. I was doing some task myself, was messing it up, and "took the name of the Lord in vain" (as we say) in my frustration. I was probably around twelve at the time, and I'm sure I thought the word was cool to say because I'd heard an adult say it.

My dad suddenly whirled around and yelled at the top of his lungs, *"Don't you ever say that again!"*

Believe me, I didn't! He was standing so close that he scared the bejeebers out of me. My father was not about to let my transgression go unchallenged. But what kid in her right mind is going to repeat an expletive in the presence of a parent? It was an innocent mistake on my part. I certainly needed to be corrected, but his reaction was way over the top for the offense and actually wounded me.

Years later, while I was working in a Mail Boxes Etc. store, a regular customer used to really unsettle me for no apparent reason. He was probably in his thirties and always looked very serious and focused on the task at hand when he came into the store. It occurred to me in later years that he looked a lot like my dad would have looked to me as a child. I was ill at ease around this customer because my emotional memory bank was telling me, *This guy could blow up at you any second now!* I had an irrational fear that told me he was going to suddenly be angry and yell. Why? I was transferring my hurt from my father's anger years before to this customer in my present because the hurt hadn't healed. In fact, if I was ever in a situation where an adult male displayed any kind of anger, I just shut down. I could not respond as a healthy adult should because the fear in me was paralyzing. I responded as the adolescent had because that's when the damage had occurred.

What I have just described to you is a fairly benign incident, yet the wound remained with me for years. How, then, can a memory of something like this—or something far worse—be healed? Through the forgiveness of sins.

"The healing of memories is the forgiveness of sins" is the way that many in the healing ministry would say it. Now, my father is not an ogre. He loved me, and he was right to correct me, but he ended up hurting me because of the way he handled the situation. Once I could see that I had an unhealed hurt from the past, I could forgive this sin against me and receive God's healing in the wounded place. I could also ask the Lord to forgive me for holding any unforgiveness against my father. I still remember the event, but it no longer controls my life in a hurtful way. The transference stopped when forgiveness was released and as the wound healed.

Here's another example of transference at work in a different way. Most summers I attend the family conference of a ministerial fellowship I belong to. I was eating lunch with a pastor friend when a man sat down at our table and introduced himself. He told us that he had come to the conference, wanting to participate, but had no means of paying for lodging.

He was actually sleeping in his tent on the facility grounds. My friend compassionately assured him that a room would be found for him to stay in for the rest of the conference. My response, however, was very different. I immediately disliked this man and increasingly grew annoyed with him the longer he sat there. I was barely civil to him, as I recall, yet I had just met him. What was wrong?

Years later, the Lord showed me that I had previously taken up an offense concerning a former neighbor of my family. Long after we'd moved away, I'd heard that this man had cheated on his wife and ended up leaving her for another woman. Since I knew the family and had even babysat his children, I was angry about what he had done. I judged him for his adultery. As it turns out, the visitor at the summer conference looked a lot like my old neighbor, and that's why I disliked him so much. I had transferred my judgment and unforgiveness toward my former neighbor to this poor man! I had an unresolved issue with someone from my past, and the visitor's physical resemblance to him triggered my sinful reaction in the present. He sat down at our table, looking for warm fellowship, and all he got from me was a cold reception. I sinned against a brother in Christ because of my failure to forgive something that neither of us was directly involved in.

I hope that these two examples illustrate that, although understandable, transference is actually a sinful and potentially damaging response rooted in our hurts and in our failure to forgive others.

As I mentioned in another chapter, time heals nothing. I want to stress this very important point again by saying it another way. The destructive power of sins committed by you or against you does not diminish with time. What we may dismiss cavalierly as "water under the bridge" is actually more like sewage backup contaminating our souls.

The fall of man was hard. Really hard. The amount of brokenness in human lives because of it is staggering to contemplate. Every sin left unconfessed, unrepented of, and therefore unforgiven in a life only continues to snowball ever larger into the future, producing more death and destruction as it grows and affecting successive generations. Even our best efforts at loving others are broken because of our fallen and unhealed condition. The only thing in the universe capable of absorbing and rendering powerless the terrible effects of sin on mankind is the body of Jesus Christ crucified.

The cross is the only remedy for our sins and the first station of healing along the path home to God. The apostle Peter gave this testimony to the God-fearing Gentiles gathered in the house of Cornelius.

> You know of Jesus of Nazareth, how God anointed Him with the Holy Spirit and with power, and how He went about doing good and healing all who were oppressed by the devil, for God was with Him. We are witnesses of all the things He did both in the land of the Jews and in Jerusalem. They also put Him to death by hanging Him on a cross. God raised Him up on the third day and granted that He become visible, not to all the people, but to witnesses who were chosen beforehand by God, that is, to us who ate and drank with Him after He arose from the dead. And He ordered us to preach to the people, and solemnly to testify that this is the One who has been appointed by God as Judge of the living and the dead. Of Him all the prophets bear witness that through His name everyone who believes in Him receives forgiveness of sins.
>
> —Acts 10:38–43

Did you get that? Everyone who believes in Jesus with her whole heart can receive the forgiveness of sins! If you can *receive* forgiveness, then you can certainly *give* forgiveness. And if you will forgive others, then you can be gloriously healed in the deepest, most wounded places of your soul. And as you are healed, you become free to grow into the person God always intended for you to become. And that is why the gospel of Jesus Christ is called the "good news." Highest praises, honor, and glory be unto His name!

Be Unto Your Name

We are a moment, You are forever,
Lord of the Ages, God before time.
We are a vapor, You are eternal,
Love everlasting, reigning on high.

Holy, holy, Lord God Almighty,
Worthy is the Lamb Who was slain!
Highest praises, honor and glory,
Be unto Your name.
Be unto Your name.

We are the broken, You are the healer,
Jesus, Redeemer, mighty to save.
You are the love song we'll sing forever,
Bowing before You, blessing Your name.

Holy, holy, Lord God Almighty,
Worthy is the Lamb Who was slain!
Highest praises, honor and glory,
Be unto Your name.
Be unto Your name.

CHAPTER EIGHT

ANCIENT WORDS

Let the word of Christ richly dwell within you, with all wisdom
teaching and admonishing one other with psalms and hymns and
spiritual songs, singing with thankfulness in your hearts to God.
                                                    —Colossians 3:16

D on't put that book on top of the Bible!"
        I froze in fear. Unwittingly, I had done the unthinkable: placing
another book on top of the Bible. I was in my fifth-grade class, and I
can still see my teacher standing beside me with fire in her eyes and an
angry flush on her cheeks. And I can still feel the humiliation of being
publicly chastised for my transgression. In the culture of my school
days, the Bible was a book to be outwardly honored, if not actually
read and taken to heart. Surely, there must be a verse in there about not
yelling at children who accidentally desecrate the Holy Writ!

Until the late 1960s, we read the Bible devotionally in the public
schools I attended. I remember sitting in my second-grade class-
room and memorizing Psalm 100. And how at a moment's notice,
any one of my classmates could recite the Golden Rule: "Do unto
others as you would have them do unto you." The moral teachings
of the Bible were a part of our public school curriculum until a
bunch of judicial activists decided it was dangerous for American
school children to be exposed to controversial ideas, such as "You

shall not steal" or "You shall not commit murder" and "Love your neighbor as yourself."

I grew up in a decidedly religious environment. My family belonged to a Methodist church, so I attended Sunday school, vacation Bible schools, and youth meetings. I endured endless hours of countless sermons and attempted to sing hymns in keys that always seemed pitched in the stratosphere. But I also saw the light of Jesus reflected in the eyes of my teachers and mentors, awakening a hunger in me to know Him as well.

During the late 1960s and early 1970s, as a wave of spiritual renewal swept the globe—and my church along with it—I came to know the love of Jesus personally and received the infilling of the Holy Spirit. Yet for all my involvement in the church, I cannot remember ever being instructed to read the Word on my own with any manner of discipline. I was a freshman in college before it occurred to me that studying the Bible was an important part of being a disciple of Jesus. How I managed to go through all those years in church without obtaining that vital piece of information, I don't know.

But I did. And when I finally began to discover the Bible for myself, it changed my life. I was set on the path of growth and maturity in my relationship with Christ. And the Scriptures became my primary inspiration as I began to write worship songs. This is especially true of one in particular, the hymn "Ancient Words."

The longer I walk with the Lord, the more love and appreciation I have for the Bible and for those whom God has used throughout the ages to make it available to me. I suppose that was the true impetus for my writing "Ancient Words." I wish I could remember exactly where I was and what I was doing when the idea introduced itself, but I cannot. I was probably doing ordinary things on an ordinary day. What I *do* remember is how compelling the idea became and how much I wanted to write it as a contemporary hymn.

Contemporary hymn—now, there are a couple of words we don't usually think of as belonging together!

Hymn is a word with a distinct meaning for many Christians. Hymns are the traditional songs we sing in our worship services, most of which were written during the last two to three centuries by the likes of Isaac Watts, Charles Wesley, and Fanny Crosby. For me, it is a word reminiscent of the Christian heritage I gained while growing up in the Methodist church.

Hymn also suggests a certain musical tradition. While the styles certainly vary, words like *classic* and *timeless* consistently come to mind. Christian songwriter and teacher Gerrit Gufstafson calls them the "redwoods" of worship music because of their enduring appeal.

On the other hand, my friend Tina would probably call them "boring." Tina didn't grow up in a traditional church and has absolutely no affection for hymns. If you mention them to her, she makes a face. But for me, *hymn* suggests roots. In this era of rapid change, something is very comforting about knowing that my faith is "rooted" in something—Someone—solid and unchanging. Relying on the Word of God for daily living is something long shared by believers. It is a part of our collective roots and connects us with the past. So it seemed fitting to me that the music and lyrical phrasing of "Ancient Words" should be that of a hymn.

But what could be contemporary about a song titled "Ancient Words," other than that it was written in 1999?

I believe an innate hunger exists in the soul of Western man to be spiritually nurtured by something older than microwave ovens. Take, for instance, the popular interest in all things Celtic. This "longing for things ancient," as Gerrit would put it, is in reality a contemporary trend. What we really long for is not just "things ancient" but a relationship with the Ancient of Days. As we read God's letter of introduction—the Bible—we discover His invitation to enter into a covenant relationship with Him and the means to walk with Him day by day. By embracing the wisdom and instruction of these ancient words, we learn how to live life as God created it to be lived.

Among the best moments in any songwriter's life is the realization that your song is a "home run". You've managed to say something in a way that deeply touches the hearts of those who hear it. For "Ancient Words," that moment came when I had the opportunity to perform at a pastors' conference of the Liberty Fellowship of Churches and Ministers.

At the time, the song had not been published, and the only recording I had of it was a simple demo. I decided to sing it for them with the accompaniment track from the demo. To say the song "went over well" would be an understatement. I was, after all, singing to a room full of preachers! But it was the reaction of one man, Jim Darnell, that convinced me that I was in "home run" territory.

Brother Jim has been part of fruitful ministry for over forty years, and he loves the Word of God. He is an avid outdoorsman, a man's man, and a preacher's preacher. I don't know whether he is easily given to tears, but that day he wept unashamedly. I was convinced that I was on to something when I was told later how deeply the song had touched him. I am so grateful to know that "Ancient Words" is an encouragement to servants of God, who, like Jim, love and teach the Scriptures with care and faithfulness.

Integrity Music was the first to record "Ancient Words." It appeared as the bonus track on a worship project recorded in 2001 with Irish worship leader Robin Mark. The setting was St. Patrick's Cathedral in Armaugh, Northern Ireland, which is "hailed as the birthplace of European Christianity," according to the liner notes from the project (titled *Come Heal This Land*). But what really gave "Ancient Words" the profile it now enjoys was when Michael W. Smith recorded it as part of his *Worship Again* CD in 2002 (another great moment in this songwriter's life).

Thanks to Robin Mark, the hymn had taken on a decidedly Celtic feel, and Michael W. Smith kept the same approach with his own beautiful arrangement. Because of the recordings of these two artists, "Ancient Words" has since become the unofficial theme song of Bible studies across our nation.

A fourth verse of "Ancient Words" was not initially recorded.

Martyrs' blood stains each page.
They have died for this faith.
Hear them cry through the years,
"Heed these words and hold them dear!"

Prior to that night of worship in the cathedral, the decision was made not to use the "martyrs' blood" verse of the song due to the ongoing political sensitivities between Irish Catholics and Protestants. Consequently, when Michael W. Smith recorded the song, this verse was again excluded, so the public is largely unaware that a fourth verse exists. In reality, when I penned this verse, I never really gave much thought to the official church persecution that oppressed those who persevered in their work of Bible translation. I was certainly aware of it, but my thoughts were motivated by the lives of the Old Testament prophets and the early Christian believers who in their day withstood so much opposition to the proclaiming of Christ's message. I see the testimony of the martyrs as covering a much broader spectrum of history than just the few centuries near the time in church history that we call the Reformation. Martyrdom for the sake of the gospel has a long history and continues, unfortunately, to the present day.

One of the unforeseen blessings of writing "Ancient Words" has been the discovery of how meaningful this song is to the men and women of Wycliffe Bible Translators.[4] These dedicated servants of God have given their lives to translating the Scriptures for the people who don't have the Word available in their native language. They spend twenty or more years of their lives in some far-flung corner of the globe so a little-known tribe of people can have, first, a written language and, second, a copy of one of the Gospels in their own tongue. It humbles me to know that a song I wrote in the relative comfort of my home has been such an inspiration and encouragement to those living so sacrificially.

One of my most prized souvenirs is a calendar published by Wycliffe Canada in 2006 that combines photographs of their work around the world with the lyrics of "Ancient Words." They even produced a music video using my own recording of the song to help present the great work they do around the world.

The fourth verse is especially meaningful to the organization that takes its name from John Wycliffe. Wycliffe is noted for overseeing an English translation of the Bible from the Latin Vulgate (circa 1380) despite official church disapproval. He wrote,

> For as much as the Bible contains Christ, that is all that is necessary for salvation, it is necessary for all men, not for priests alone.[5]

It was his strong conviction as well as the conviction of the organization bearing his name that everyone should be able to read the Scriptures in their own language.

Amen to that!

Ancient Words

Holy words long preserved,
For our walk in this world.
They resound with God's own heart.
O let the ancient words impart.

Words of life, words of hope,
Give us strength, help us cope.
In this world, where e'er we roam,
Ancient words will guide us home.

Ancient words, ever true,
Changing me and changing you.
We have come with open hearts.
O let the ancient words impart.

Holy words of our faith,
Handed down to this age.
Came to us through sacrifice.
O heed the faithful word of Christ!

Martyrs' blood stains each page.
They have died for this faith.
Hear them cry through the years,
"Heed these words and hold them dear!"

ANCIENT WORDS

Ancient words, ever true,
Changing me and changing you,
We have come with open hearts.
O let the ancient words impart.

Words and music by Lynn DeShazo
© 2001 Integrity's Hosanna! Music/ASCAP.
All rights reserved. Lyrics reprinted by permission.

CHAPTER NINE

THE DIAMOND
TURNS

*To me, the very least of all saints, this grace was given, to preach
to the Gentiles the unfathomable riches of Christ, and to bring to
light what is the administration of the mystery which for ages has
been hidden in God who created all things; so that the manifold
wisdom of God might now be made known through the church
to the rulers and the authorities in the heavenly places.*
—Ephesians 3:8–10

One of my favorite quotes about songwriting is from Sheila Davis, author of several excellent books on the subject.

"Unlike a poem," she pens in *The Craft of Lyric Writing*, "whose language can be as abstract as a cubist painting, a lyric should be as direct as a highway sign."[6]

In other words, a song lyric should be clearly understood by the listener.

In 2000 I wrote a song that has raised a question from a few people. They wonder about the phrase "the diamond turns."

The trouble with writing about divine mystery is that it's hard not to seem so . . . well, mysterious! I'll have to admit, "the diamond turns" is a bit of a stretch for some church folks to understand at first. But how does anyone describe such awe-inspiring things without at least a hint of the mystery one is writing of?

As a songwriter, I work much like a painter. Except that I create images with words and music instead of with oils and watercolors. I used this mysterious-sounding phrase as a metaphor for the ever-unfolding revelation of God's glory and holiness.

Many people understand the concept of the diamond right away. Yet others don't. Maybe they've never spent much time reading the Old Testament prophets or the book of Revelation. Maybe they are just "right-brain challenged"; I don't know.

(If you want to know the truth, I realize that not everyone sees things the way I do. But the lack of imagination in some people just irks me!)

The idea for "The Diamond Turns" came to me in the fall of 1999 during a class lecture on the book of Ephesians. Our instructor, Dr. Jay Ferguson, was teaching on Paul's description of God's wisdom in Ephesians 3:10 as being *polupoikilos*. This Greek word is rendered in English as "manifold," meaning that it has many sides or colors. "Multifaceted" is another word that can be used.

To demonstrate, Dr. Ferguson gave us the illustration of a diamond. If you hold up a diamond to the light and view it in one position, you will be able to see several of its facets. If you turn the diamond slightly, even more of its beauty and brilliance can be seen.

Dr. Ferguson described to the class what it must be like for the heavenly beings around God's throne as they continually behold the ever-unfolding revelation of His glory. They cry, "Holy!" as they see a glorious dimension of the Lord. They cry, "Holy!" again as another facet of His glory is revealed, much like the turning of a diamond. A third time they cry, "Holy!" to still another revelation of His glory.[7] And on and on it goes so "day and night they do not cease to say 'Holy, holy, holy is the Lord God, the Almighty, who was and who is and who is to come'" (Rev. 4:8).

As I pondered this image of heavenly worship before God's throne, his description of the turning diamond captured my imagination. I scribbled a few lines of a song idea in the margin of my notes and tried to concentrate on the rest of the lecture.

> The diamond turns, the angels bow
> Holy, holy, holy is the Lord!

According to Paul's letter to the Ephesians, God's manifold wisdom has been "made known through the church to the rulers and the authorities in the heavenly places" (Eph. 3:10). What the apostle is saying is that the powers to whom God is demonstrating His wisdom and grace are the beings that rebelled against Him and the very ones we constantly struggle against in this life.[8]

In *The Book of Ephesians Course Study Guide* syllabus, Dr. Ferguson states,

> Every sentient being God has ever created will exist forever, either with God in heaven or in "the lake of fire that burns forever." No ruler, authority, power or any other kind of spirit will ever be able to accuse God of being unloving, unkind, or unforgiving. The eternal proof of His grace and kindness will be seated and reigning with His Son! The proof of God's loving kindness is us, the church, the children of God! The church is the trophy of God's complete victory and the evidence of His grace to all of the rulers and authorities that rebelled against Him!

Later, I reflected on words from the apostle Paul to the church in Corinth, planted in the heart of the Gentile world so rife with Hellenistic thought and "wisdom."

> Yet we do speak wisdom among those who are mature; a wisdom, however, not of this age nor of the rulers of this age, who are passing away; but we speak God's wisdom in a mystery, the hidden wisdom which God predestined before the ages to our glory; the wisdom which none of the rulers of this age has understood; for if they had understood it they would not have crucified the Lord of glory.
> —1 Corinthians 2:6–8

All that theological "food for thought" eventually distilled into the song's bridge.

> Who can stand, O Lord, before Your eyes of fire
> Or speak against the wisdom You've reflected in Your bride . . .

It wasn't until August 2000 that I finished writing "The Diamond Turns." I don't recall why it took the better part of a year to compose. Every song has its own gestation period, I suppose. The more substantial the idea, the longer it seems to take me to bring it to birth, creatively speaking. I recorded the song on my CD by the same title in 2001. It was also recorded "live" in September 2001 at the World Prayer Center in Colorado Springs during a songwriters' recording for Integrity Music on the CD *Hope of the Nations.*

As it turned out, the Colorado Springs recording came within just a couple of weeks of the now-infamous terrorist attacks on the World Trade Towers and the Pentagon on September 11, 2001. A lot of previously planned events were canceled during the uncertain days that followed those attacks, but the night of worship at the World Prayer Center went on as planned. I was so glad to be in a place where God's people had gathered, to be a part of praising and worshipping Him with all our hearts, and to pray for the nations during this tumultuous time.

Each songwriter participating in the evening of worship performed two of his or her own songs, leading the assembly gathered in the World Prayer Center in praise and worship. I was scheduled to go on somewhere just after the midpoint of the evening. When my turn came, I started with "The Diamond Turns." For me, sometimes leading worship is like flying by instruments. I don't feel the presence of God; I just trust that He is there. But this particular occasion was like approaching the holy of holies itself. As the song began, the atmosphere of the gathering began to change markedly. It felt to me as though God had just walked into the room; the air itself was charged with His glory!

It is always awkward for me to comment on my own worship leading, so I will quote from a very gracious note written to me later by one of the backing vocalists who sang the entire evening.

> That night in Colorado Springs was so great to be a part of, but sensing the anointing of the Spirit on you, and experiencing the presence of the Lord when you sang and then prophesied . . . well, I was moved to tears. The presence of God was tangible. You really ushered Him in.

My sharing a note such as this one is not meant to elevate my position as a songwriter. But sometimes worship leaders need encouragement; the whole point of what we do is to help make a way for God's people to encounter His presence as they worship Him, and it's nice to know when we have done that.

I know that I had very little to do with God's choice to manifest Himself to us so powerfully that evening. I was only one of a dozen or so gifted worship leaders who participated that night. But it was enormously affirming to me to realize that I had touched on heavenly realities in the writing of this song and that God Himself seemed to give the "amen." He drew near to us in such a glorious way as we revered Him in worship and declared afresh to men and angels—even to powers and principalities—the awesome reality of His glory, His holiness, and His manifold wisdom. And that wisdom in the end triumphantly prevails over the worst evil that wicked men or demons can perpetrate against those who belong to the Almighty.

After I began writing this book, I learned that "The Diamond Turns" was scheduled to be recorded last year (2009) by Integrity Music recording artist Paul Wilbur. Paul is an anointed worship leader, a Messianic Jewish believer, and he definitely "gets it!"

The Diamond Turns

Who is like You, O Lord among gods?
Who can but worship as You shine?
Who could ever know in just a single gaze,
All the glory of Your face?
All the glory of Your face?

The diamond turns, the angels bow.
Holy, holy, holy is the Lord!
The Glory burns, the saints cry out,
Holy, holy, holy is the Lord!
Holy, holy, holy is the Lord!

Who is there like You, O radiant One,
Ever exceeding all we know?
Merciful and just, full of grace and love.
Ever shining from Your throne.
Ever shining from Your throne.

The diamond turns, the angels bow.
Holy, holy, holy is the Lord!
The Glory burns, the saints cry out,
Holy, holy, holy is the Lord!
Holy, holy, holy is the Lord!

Who can stand, O Lord, before Your eyes of fire?
Or speak against the wisdom You've reflected
in Your bride?
We fall upon our knees and join the ancient cry,
Holy, holy, holy is the Lord Most High!
Holy, holy, holy is the Lord!
Holy, holy, holy!

The diamond turns.

CHAPTER TEN

LEARN TO LOVE

*Love is patient, love is kind and is not jealous; love does not brag and
is not arrogant, does not act unbecomingly; it does not seek its own,
is not provoked, does not take into account a wrong suffered, does not
rejoice with unrighteousness, but rejoices with the truth; bears all things,
believes all things, hopes all things, endures all things. Love never fails.*
—1 Corinthians 13:4–8a

*But the goal of our instruction is love from a pure heart and
a good conscience and a sincere faith.*
—1 Timothy 1:5

I've ministered as a worship leader in a lot of different places over
the years—local churches, retreats, conferences, prisons, evangelistic
outreaches, charitable fund-raisers, weddings, and funerals. I've sung
in about half of our fifty states and in a number of other countries. I
even sang for a tank battalion on an Israeli military base with my tour
group joining in. Somewhere in the middle of "The Battle Belongs
to the Lord,"[9] it suddenly dawned on me that, just like the Levitical
singers of King Jehoshaphat's day, I was singing God's praises before
the armies of Israel. *Literally!*

Most of my ministry experiences have been spiritually rewarding
and well worth the challenges to go through them. I'm glad I said yes
to those opportunities, even if the only fruit that came from them was

a personal lesson learned. Then there's the handful of things I'd like to forget about entirely. They are filed in my memory bank under *What was I thinking?*

One particular experience, however, I don't think I'll ever be able to forget, nor do I wish to. On July 13, 2000, I sang for the memorial service of a precious mentally handicapped woman named Della Evelyn Cobern, fondly known by all who loved her as "Ms. Ev." It was genuinely one of the most extraordinary privileges of my life.

Ms. Ev is the sister of my friend Valeta Bush, also known to her friends as "Bunny." As she tells it, her husband started calling her "Honey Bunny," and the name stuck. Ed and Bunny oversee a Christian residential ministry called Wellspring for Women, which they started in 1984. The Lord spoke to them about providing a place for hurting girls to come to rebuild their lives in a loving, yet disciplined Christian environment. In obedience, the Bushes opened their rural Marbury, Alabama, home to several girls. A couple of years later, Ms. Ev came to join them. Ms. Ev, you see, had spent the previous forty-four years of her life in the state mental hospital.

Now all of their lives would change forever.

I first had the occasion to get to know Ms. Ev when I ministered to the ladies living at Wellspring. Bunny told me a lot about her during my visits there, so I was already familiar with her story on the day of her funeral. I knew, for example, what a handful she could be. I'd seen the large hole she made in the back of one of Bunny's dining room chairs; it looked like a bomb had gone off! I also knew she had to be watched carefully because she could disappear at the drop of a hat. In spite of all the challenges, Bunny had chosen to be her caregiver for the last fourteen years.

I was, not surprisingly, deeply moved by the testimony of Ms. Ev's life, as given by her sister in the eulogy. So moved, in fact, that I asked Bunny for a copy of it. But I was totally unprepared for what God would speak to me before the memorial service began.

I considered how best to recount Ms. Ev's extraordinary life. Surely I could just draw on what Bunny had so tenderly written and give the important highlights. Her story, however, begs to be told in its entirety. And who better to tell it than her own sister and caregiver? So here is Ms. Ev's eulogy, edited only slightly.

Eulogy for Della Evelyn Cobern
by Valeta Bush

We have come this afternoon to glorify the Lord Jesus Christ for His Love, His Grace and Mercy, and His life-changing power in the life of Della Evelyn Cobern, affectionately called "Ms. Ev" by those who knew her in the last fourteen years. Any who knew of her life could not help but know that there is a God who loves us with an unfathomable love and who will turn heaven and earth upside down to answer prayers, honor His Word, and bless His children.

Ms. Ev was born June 23, 1924, the second child born to Charles Jefferson and Lida Carroll Cobern. She was specially planned by God with a mission and a destiny. Her life was not lived in vain, although to the ordinary eye she seemed like a mistake. I believe she fulfilled her calling from God and will hear her Father say, "Well done, thy good and faithful servant; enter into the joy of the Lord."

Ms. Ev saw hard times as a child, living through a time of great privation during the Great Depression. She was the second of six children with an older brother Carroll and four sisters—Christine, Lilly, Alice, and Valeta. All except Christine and I preceded her into eternity, and I can imagine the reunion she is having with them now in glory, clothed in her right mind and free from all encumbrances of earth and flesh. Her mother, a godly woman, taught her children about God and prayed for them through a difficult home situation. Little Evelyn suffered most, having been born mentally retarded and showing signs of emotional disorders at an early age.

Even so, she did complete nine grades in school, being given a lot of grace by the school system in the small rural community of Maplesville, Alabama, where she grew up. Moving to Montgomery, Alabama, as a teenager was particularly traumatic to her. She could not keep up in school, and there were no special education classes in those days. The school suggested she be withdrawn.

Ms. Ev exhibited a lot of self-hatred and destructive behavior from childhood, destroying all pictures she found of herself. She was combative, angry, and confused. She ran away frequently and hid herself for days at a time. One time she hitched a freight and ended up in New York. The authorities found her and returned her. That was when the doctors told Mom and Dad that there was no hope for her. They said she needed to be institutionalized to keep her from hurting herself and others. Not knowing any other solution, her parents followed their advice. Ms. Ev was nineteen years old.

The next forty-four years would prove to be a nightmare for her. She was separated from her family, the only love she knew. Most people slowly forgot about her, perhaps trying to deal with the pain they felt. Her mom, dad, and sisters did not, though. Faithful trips, shopping tours, picnics, luncheons out, special gifts, and letters from family were attempts to keep her close in spirit. The hospital started therapy using high dosages of strong mind-altering drugs and shock treatments. I remember as a child seeing her beg Mom to make them stop. Mom would talk to the doctors, and they would reassure her that this was the only way to treat her disorder.

Ms. Ev gave the hospital a run for their money and kept us all hopping, though. She escaped the hospital numerous times. One time on a family outing, she opened the car door and stepped out into four lanes of traffic as the car drew to a stop at a red light. Another time she asked to go to a park and wound up jumping from a high bluff into a river. On this and many other occasions, God was watching out for her through the prayers of her mother and sisters.

On a visit with her in 1973, I was eager to share my new life in Christ Jesus. I wanted to see her saved, healed, delivered, and Spirit-filled! After I shared with her, she let me know that the Lord had beaten me to the draw. While watching Billy Graham on television at the hospital, she responded to his altar call when he invited the people watching by television to lay their hands on the TV and pray with him in their hearts to receive Jesus as their Savior, as thousands streamed forward in the arena to do the same. She told me with excitement, "I did! And I felt a warm feeling all over my body. I ask God if He would get me out of this place!"

Not long afterward, we tried to help God answer her prayers. We took her out of the hospital to try keeping her at home. But after two and a half months it was obvious that she could not make it outside the hospital at this time. She did get her first airplane ride, though, when her sister Chris paid her way to fly to Atlanta for a two week visit. She never forgot that ride; it was the highlight of her life! She was baptized while in Atlanta, too, and reaffirmed her faith in the Lord. Returning her to the hospital was heart wrenching. She was really set back by it, but when the Lord got ready for her to come home, the doors opened easily and readily.

In 1986, Ms. Ev was placed in a foster home. She had been placed several times before and always wound up going back to the hospital. This time, it soon became apparent that she was not being adequately cared for. After talking with my husband, Ed, and other family members, I moved to get legal custody, which was swiftly granted. She came to live with the Bush family and her eighty-six-year-old mother, who had come to live with us the previous year. Family reunion! And healing! Mom and Ms. Ev shared a room, and we saw some tender moments. We also saw some hair-pulling fights!

In 1984, God told us to begin a ministry for hurting girls and women. By the time Mom and Ms. Ev arrived, we also had several girls living in the house with us. We were one *big* family! Mom and Ms. Ev were, for the most part, readily loved and accepted by the girls. The girls were able to laugh off the funny and often embarrassing things that happened. Both sides were getting, after all, what they needed most—lots of love and attention. Mom and Ms. Ev both had an assignment from God in the ministry here. We all began to learn through them about the unconditional love of God, humility, gentle-ness, kindness, and about preferring others above ourselves.

Ms. Ev started the habit of calling everyone "Hon." I still do it today. She sang with all her heart the old hymns of the church. Her favorite was "The Old Rugged Cross," which she would sing loudly, changing the lyrics according to the way she heard them. I don't know if I will ever be able to sing it correctly again! She was in every church service as long as she was able. Sometimes she would preach louder than Pastor Ed and have to be removed from the service.

Wherever we went, she and Mom would go with us, for as long as they were physically able. Sometimes Ms. Ev would go when you didn't want her to. She could disappear in a flash. Living out here in the middle of nowhere, we would not know in what direction to look. The rescue squad would have to be called out, and it would sometimes take hours to find her. That's when having a church family and a ministry to young women was so comforting and rewarding. Prayer and faith in God would see her safely home and sustain the family through the crisis. Ms. Ev drew us into a deeper relationship with God because we had to rely totally upon *Him* in dealing with *her!*

The most miraculous of our episodes was the one in which we would see the dead raised to life. On December 26, 1992, Ms. Ev decided to leave the house sometime after 2:00 AM— we heard her get up to go to the bathroom around that time. She was discovered about 8:00 AM the next morning with *no vital signs*, clothed in only a hospital gown in nearly freezing temperatures. Prayer warriors on staff, in the church, and among the students began to pray. We never entertained the idea that she was dead. We took off to the hospital where, upon our arrival, they immediately began to try to bring her body temperature up from 73 degrees and to get her pulse and breathing restored. The cardiologist who was called in told us it was hopeless. He had never seen anyone survive with a body temperature that low. Even if she could be resuscitated, she would be a vegetable. He encouraged us to let her go.

I could get no peace about that decision, but I wanted God's will for her. God was already on the scene, getting a number of our friends to the hospital just at the right time to join together with me in prayer. About the time we finished, there was a stirring in the area where a medical team had been taking turns for over three hours as they tried to get Ms. Ev's vitals back. The doctor quickly came to tell us that she had a pulse, she was breathing on her own, and her body temp had risen five degrees. She was alive! Police arrived about that time, wanting me to tell them about the circumstances of her death. They were very apologetic when I told them she wasn't dead!

The next day and a half were touch and go. The doctor was still very skeptical. The Lord told me on the day I got to see her to claim Psalm 23 for her, so that became my prayer, meditation, and my faith confession from that time on. The nurse greeted us with the good news that she thought she'd seen some response from Ms. Ev. Her frail, little body was hooked up to all kinds of tubes and machines, and she looked pathetic. I walked to the side of the bed and spoke to her. Her eyes flew open, and even with tubes everywhere, preventing speech, she showed me with her eyes that she knew me and was awfully glad to see me. Later when Michael, my son, and Richard, my son-in-law, came back to the unit, I said, "Ms. Ev, Michael is here," and she turned her head to look straight at him and smile! From that day, I called her "my little tomato" since the doctor said she'd be a vegetable!

One night I came into the hospital room to find her with her hand in the air and pointed toward the left corner of the room. I said, "Whatcha doin', Ms. Ev?"

She said, "I see Him! He's right there!"

"Who?" I asked, though I felt certain I knew from the expression on her face. "Is it Jesus?"

"Jesus," she replied, with a voice distorted by weeks with tubes down her throat. Although I could not see what she saw, I felt His presence giving peace and filling the room with His comfort and love.

Ms. Ev's recovery was slow but steady. She learned to walk, to eat, to tie her shoes and dress herself, and to bathe herself. She was doing things she hadn't done before the accident.

Once she was released from the hospital, we tried to let Ms. Ev experience life as she had never been able to before. She loved to dress up, and "Go" was her middle name. We took her swimming and she had a ball! She went boating, had two more plane rides, and even rode a horse with the help of Rachelle, one of our former students. I bought her an adult-sized tricycle because she loved to bike—she taught me!—but she was never able to negotiate it successfully. We took her on trips, especially to Callaway Gardens, Georgia. Until the last year of her life, she always seemed to enjoy herself. Her favorite thing was eating. She was a little thing, but she could eat like a construction worker!

In the last two years, I began to let Ms. Ev miss our evening church services. She seemed more restless and fractious in the evenings, and I didn't want her to disrupt services. We would check on her periodically, leaving her to watch Christian television. One evening I went into the kitchen where she was watching the TV to discover her with both hands and her head raised to heaven and talking in a language I had never heard from her, although sometimes her speech did sound funny. She wasn't distracted by me at all, so I just left her alone. I felt like I was intruding upon a private conversation.

I don't know of a single soul who knew her who was not impacted by her life. People learned about God's love simply by seeing it demonstrated so keenly upon Ms. Ev. She gave people hope. And she worked on our flesh diligently! If we were going to have a relationship with God, it was obvious that we would have to learn to walk in 1 Corinthians 13:4–8 *Amplified* with Ms. Ev. Nothing else would do! She gave to those who deeply needed to be needed, and she helped give them a sense of belonging and self-worth. She was therapy to us all.

I always believed Ms. Ev was a special gift of God sent to this ministry to touch the lives of our women and to teach them about Himself. But I will never forget when it finally dawned upon me that her particular calling was to develop the character of Jesus *in me!* I was learning reams about the love of God and the value of life to Him. I was also learning that every person, no matter how insignificant he or she might seem to the world, has a special calling from God, a special purpose and design. As my heart began to change in this crucible of love, I began to discover what the abundant life that Jesus came to bring us is all about. I began to have greater insight into the sufferings and feelings of infirmity in others. I became more conscious of investing my life in others in order to improve life for them and to help them fulfill their goals and dreams.

In the last week, Ms. Ev began to show a marked decline. She was having difficulty sitting up, and her foot became swollen. Lisa, my right-hand girl who helped me with Ms. Ev for several months, assisted in getting her to the doctor, who told me he suspected a blood clot. We followed his instructions, which included total bed rest and elevating her foot. The swelling began to go down, but she lost the ability to swallow, and we were having difficulty even getting fluids into her. Last Saturday night, after Lisa helped me get her ready for bed, I felt a heaviness in my heart and a need to pray differently for Ms. Ev. I found myself praying a prayer of release. I asked the Lord to completely heal her if her mission on earth was not finished. I then added that I released her into His will if she was ready to go home with Him. I asked for three things through my tears. One, that she would not have to go to an impersonal hospital where they would separate her from her family, as they had done with Mom. Two, that she would not have a long, drawn out, painful struggle but would pass quietly and peacefully into His arms. And three, that I would be with her when she left.

The following Tuesday morning—my birthday—I went downstairs at 6:30 to get Ms. Ev ready to go to the doctor again to see what we could do to get nourishment into her. I fully expected to have to hospitalize her. As I went into her room, I was pleasantly surprised to find her sleeping very peacefully with none of the incessant jerking that had become so characteristic of her over the last few months. I bathed her face and hands and swabbed out her mouth, but she seemed undisturbed. Lisa arrived to help me dress her. She still continued to rest quietly. We took her to the kitchen, and she took several swallows of juice offered her through a straw; we were encouraged. Suddenly, her steady breathing became very shallow, and in a moment's time, she slipped quietly and peacefully into glory with my hands embracing her face—all three requests granted! What a wonderful birthday present to me from a loving Father!

As the news of her home going spread, calls began to come in from students who had known and loved Ms. Ev. Many of them had been close to her, watching her for me when I needed to take care of other things. All of them expressed how much Ms. Ev had meant to them and how she was a factor in changing their lives forever.

Lord, sometimes Your gifts to us come packaged in a way that belies their worth. Ms. Ev was our special gift of love from our loving Father. Thank You, Lord, for sharing her with us and using her to train us up in holiness and god-liness. Her work is done. Enter into the joy of the Lord, beloved sister! Say "hello" to the others for us. We'll see you again, sooner than any of us think.[10]

There wasn't a dry eye in the chapel by the time Bunny finished. Mine really hadn't been since the moment I drove onto the property about an hour earlier. As I parked my car near the chapel, I saw that the family was just returning from a private graveside service. I stepped out of the car to greet them, right into a very tangible sense of the Lord's presence. Then I heard Him speak to me. *There's an anointing at the place of sacrifice.*

I say that I heard Him, but the experience was more like feeling the enormity of His words upon my heart. And I knew in that moment that He was teaching me an important principle, one that explained why Jesus' earthly ministry was so effective and why the preaching of the cross will always have the power to change lives.

I have always admired the work that Ed and Bunny do out at Wellspring.[11] Years ago they offered God all that they had, even their personal home, and asked Him to use them in His service. God took them up on it, and they've never looked back. As a result of their sacrifice, countless people have been changed by the power of God's love. As I entered the small chapel, the Lord's words still fresh in my spirit, I realized why so many women have found healing love and restoring grace during their time at Wellspring. If there's a powerful anointing flowing out of Ed and Bunny Bush to love women and see their lives restored—and there is—it's because there's a place of sacrifice in their lives for it to flow out of. They gave their lives completely to God and His purposes for them. They offered Him all the resources they had to help the hurting women who come through their doors. Perhaps most precious of all, though, was the sacrifice that made room in their busy lives and demanding ministry for Ms. Ev. I can't help but think that the Lord must surely see it that way.

> "Teacher, which is the great commandment in the Law?" And He said to him, "'You shall love the Lord Your God with all your heart, and with all your soul, and with all your mind.' This is the great and foremost commandment. The second is like it, 'You shall love your neighbor as yourself.' On these two commandments depend the whole Law and the Prophets."
>
> —Matthew 22:36–40

In God's eyes, everything hinges on love. If I accomplish the tasks of ministry but fail to love someone in the process, then I have failed. Period. I've failed a lot, quite honestly. I still have so much to learn about loving others. But to walk with God is to learn to love, so I have hope. And I am inspired by the example of people like Ed and Bunny Bush, who have shown me what God can do through the ordinary lives of those who choose the "more excellent way"[12] of love.

Learn to Love

At the end of days, when there is no more,
Of our earthly ways, of strife and war,
When Jesus stands among His own,
He will ask us there, did we learn to love?

When He looks at me with searching eyes,
Will I meet His gaze, will I laugh or cry?
When His holy flame touches all my works,
Will gold remain or will they burn?

Jesus, Jesus, faithful and true,
Jesus, Jesus, help me love like You.

There are very few important things,
And of the few, only this, my King,
That I follow You as You teach me, Lord,
How to live my life and to learn to love.

Jesus, Jesus, faithful and true,
Jesus, Jesus, help me love like You.

When You come again in Your glory, Lord,
When You appear with Your reward,
When I give account for the deeds I've done,
May I answer well, "Yes, I learned to love!"

When I give account for the deeds I've done,
May I answer well, "Yes, I learned to love!"

Words and music by Lynn DeShazo
© 2005 Integrity's Hosanna! Music/ASCAP
All rights reserved. Lyrics reprinted by permission.

CHAPTER ELEVEN

THE GATES OF ZION

The Lord loves the gates of Zion more than all the other dwelling places of Jacob.
Glorious things are spoken of you, O city of God.
—Psalm 87:2–3

If I ever visit Israel again, I don't think I'll go as part of a tour. I've been twice, and both times I spent the last day in bed, sick and exhausted, while the rest of my group shopped in Jerusalem and visited favorite places at their leisure. Tours of Israel are usually designed to take in as much as possible, and the pace is ridiculous. There's often only a frustratingly limited amount of time to spend in a scheduled stop. You get to "walk where Jesus walked" all right, but you speed through in about eight days what the Lord took three and half years of ministry to cover!

The first time I traveled to Israel was in November 2001, just weeks after 9/11. Eerily, the day-month format noted our November 9 arrival into the country as 9/11/2001. Tourism in Israel was almost nonexistent during our stay because of the *intifada*. (*Intifada* is the Arabic word for "throwing off" and is the name given to the organized violence against the Jews in the land of Israel.)

In September 2000 the *intifada* had kicked up afresh. Add to that the terrorist attack on the World Trade Towers and the Pentagon, and most American Christians were not too interested in touring the Holy Land that fall. So during my first-ever tour of Israel, conducted by my friends Dee and Carlton Baxter, our intrepid group of twenty-four had practically every place we visited to ourselves. When I visited Israel with the Baxters in 2004, things were quite different. Tourism was flourishing again, and our group's biggest challenge was getting to the next stop on our tour before part of the one-thousand-person Benny Hinn group showed up!

Well, that's not quite true. Our biggest challenge was navigating Jerusalem in a tour bus right after Yasser Arafat died in a French hospital. Arafat was the controversial leader of the Palestinian Liberation Organization. He was a lifelong terrorist against the Jews and a real pain in the behind both to Israel and the rest of the world. He died in the early hours of November 11, the day we departed the Dead Sea for Jerusalem. Consequently, Israeli security was tighter than the bark on a tree, and the tension in the city was palpable.

Jerusalem is no stranger to tension and conflict. Over the course of its three-thousand-year history, the city has changed hands numerous times. By one account it was razed to the ground sixteen times and rebuilt seventeen times.[13] In antiquity, Jerusalem was the Jebusite mountain fortress captured by King David, who made it his home and the capital city of the ancient kingdom of Israel. In the Scriptures, Jerusalem is known by about seventy names, including the City of David, the City of God, and the Holy Mountain. Most commonly, however, it is called "Zion." Under David and Solomon the city became the worship center of the Jewish nation and remained so as long as the Jews inhabited the land of Israel. In times of captivity and exile, the hope of the Jewish people was always to return to their land and to worship the Lord once again in Jerusalem.

Jerusalem is not only a treasured geographical place to the Jewish people but also a primary symbol of their hopes and aspirations as a people. The prophets often mentioned Zion when they spoke of the messianic kingdom that was to come.

> And many peoples will come and say, "Come, let us go up to the mountain of the Lord, to the house of the God of Jacob; that He may teach us His concerning His ways and that we may walk in His paths." For the law will go forth from Zion and the word of the Lord from Jerusalem.
> —Isaiah 2:3

Other groups lay claim to Jerusalem, of course, most notably Christians and Muslims. One fact is crystal clear from the Scriptures though: Jerusalem belongs to God.

> But I have chosen Jerusalem that My name might be there.
> —2 Chronicles 6:6a

> For the Lord has chosen Zion; He has desired it for His habitation. "This is My resting place forever; Here I will dwell, for I have desired it."
> —Psalm 132:13–14

And because God Himself lays claim to it, there is yet another important symbolism in this city. The Bible narratives concerning Jerusalem paint a powerful picture for us of God's dealings in the lives of His people and of the individual believer. The book of Nehemiah is a prime example.

If you know anything about the history of ancient Israel, you know that as long as its residents obeyed the Lord and held to His commandment to let the land lie fallow every seventh year, they prospered. If they disobeyed, however, they were destroyed by invaders and forcibly removed from the land, as the Lord's judgment against them.[14]

The commandment to observe the sabbatical year was not some obscure agricultural ordinance for an ancient people. God had a very compassionate reason for this commandment.

> You shall sow your land for six years and gather in its yield, but on the seventh year you shall let it rest and lie fallow, so that the needy of your people may eat; and whatever they leave the beast of the field may eat. You are to do the same with your vineyard and your olive grove.
> —Exodus 23:10–11

When Israel failed to let their fields rest every seventh year, the poorest and most powerless among them suffered. Their already difficult lives were made worse because God's provision was withheld from them. In God's eyes, this was a grave injustice. In addition, God had instructed Israel not to worship the gods of the nations around them.

Canaanite religion was steeped in the Baal cult with its perverse sexual practices and child sacrifice. God would surely cast Israel out of the land if they participated in such abominations.

True to the warning, God's righteous judgment fell upon the offending nation. In 722 BC, the Assyrians attacked the northern kingdom of Israel.[15] A forced march out of the land ensued, and historians are still uncertain where those ten tribes are today. In 586 BC, the Babylonian Empire attacked the southern kingdom of Judah, and the people were taken away to Babylon in three waves. It would be a seventy-year exile, one year for every year that Israel should have allowed the land to rest. Worst of all, the city of Jerusalem, with its magnificent temple built by King Solomon, was destroyed by the invading army and left in ruins. Interestingly, only a handful of the poorest Jews remained to eke out whatever subsistence they could from the fields and vineyards the Babylonians left to them.[16]

In the twentieth year of King Artaxerxes, Nehemiah was serving as cupbearer to the king in the capitol city of Susa. But his heart was in Zion. Nehemiah learned that things back home were not very good at all, and he was heartbroken by his countrymen's report of the devastation.

> They said to me, "The remnant there in the province who survived the captivity are in great distress and reproach, and the wall of Jerusalem is broken down and its gates are burned with fire." When I heard these words, I sat down and wept and mourned for days; and I was fasting and praying before the God of heaven.
>
> —Nehemiah 1:3–4

Nehemiah was so burdened by the plight of the Jews and the condition of Jerusalem that he undertook a bold plan to return there and do what he could for the people and the city. The book of Nehemiah tells his inspiring account of the difficult work to restore the wall and gates of the beloved city and to encourage its demoralized inhabitants.

When Nehemiah finally arrived to see the condition of Jerusalem for himself, it confirmed his worst fears. But Nehemiah was a man on a mission. After a covert inspection of the city walls and gates in the dark of night, he spoke to the Jewish leaders there and issued a challenge.

> You see the bad situation we are in, that Jerusalem is desolate and its gates burned by fire. Come, let us rebuild the wall of Jerusalem so that we will no longer be a reproach.
>
> —Nehemiah 2:17

Nehemiah did find one encouraging development though. The temple of the Lord had been rebuilt a few years before under Zerubbabel, though not as gloriously as King Solomon's original one. Temple worship had recently resumed in Jerusalem, and Ezra the priest had arranged to return from Babylon. He immediately busied himself teaching Israel again the laws of God and making them repent and return to His righteous standards.[17]

When anyone repents of his sins and comes to the Lord for salvation, a marvelous thing happens. Once "dead in your trespasses and sins" (Eph. 2:1), you are made "alive together with Christ" (Eph. 2:5) and become a "new creature" (2 Cor. 5:17). The Spirit of God comes to fill the temple of your body. There's a light in your eyes that wasn't there before because the Light of the World has made His dwelling within you. As in Ezra's day, the light is on in your "temple," and worship is arising to God. Your spirit is alive and well, and what you have experienced is glorious. Truly a miracle.

Hallelujah! Amen!

"And they all lived happily ever after."

End of story, right?

Now that you've experienced the new birth, you're suddenly a perfect model of righteous behavior and godly attitudes. You're never afraid of anyone or anything. You always do the right thing in every situation. You love everyone unconditionally. You never get mad or irritated with family members or perfect strangers. You never fall back into your old habits or let your appetites get the best of you, and . . .

Well, this is now an obviously tongue-in-cheek assessment of your experience to date, isn't it? The reality of growing as a Christian is that salvation occurs in an instant, but transformation takes time.

The book of Nehemiah magnificently parallels the condition of the lives of many Christians today. They have a genuine spiritual life, but their souls are still in ruins. They often seem powerless to appropriate the power of Christ to change their lives. They are like the men of Judah in Nehemiah's day.

> The strength of the burden bearers is failing, yet there is much rubbish; and we ourselves are unable to rebuild the wall.
>
> —Nehemiah 4:10

A large disparity often exists between the life we know we should be experiencing as Christians and the one we actually have. Our inner conversations about ourselves might go something like this:

> "I'm supposed to live differently from people who don't know Jesus, aren't I?"

Yes, indeed!

> "Now that I'm a Christian, my life should be better now, shouldn't it?"

Definitely.

> "I've been a believer for about twenty years now. I should be full of the joy of the Lord and experiencing more of 'the victorious Christian life,' shouldn't I?"

Yes, one would think so.

> "But I'm not. Not really. Oh, I put on a good face for my friends. Truth is, though, I can't shake this depression."

Or "I still have nightmares sometimes. I'm thirty-two years old, and I'm afraid to go to sleep without a light on."

Or "My wife is becoming just like my mother, and it's driving me crazy! The Bible says God hates divorce, but I've been thinking about it a lot lately."

Or "Every time I close my eyes at night, I see the war. I started drinking to help me sleep; I just don't tell my church friends."

Or "I know what the Bible says about homosexuality, but I've always felt attracted to other women (or men), and I can't seem to help myself. I would die if anyone knew I struggled with this."

Or "I can't stop watching porn. I know it's wrong, but I can't stop, and I'm too ashamed to admit it to anybody. I know God hates sin. Does God hate me?"

And on and on. The landscape of Zion looks pretty desolate, doesn't it? Why do some people who profess to know Jesus as their Savior still struggle with such things? What's wrong here?

Nehemiah has an answer for us.

> The wall of Jerusalem is broken down and its gates are burned with fire.
>
> —Nehemiah 1:3

Walls protect and secure what lies within them. They keep destructive things out, like wild beasts, marauders, and invading armies. The gates of a city are the place where decisions are rendered and judgments are made. Gates are designed to open to the good things and close to the bad. In the life of a human being, walls represent the soul—identity and the boundaries of one's personhood—and gates represent the decision-making capacity of the will, to use the analogy of Nehemiah. When they're in good repair, they function as they were meant to. If they've been damaged, however, the person is vulnerable to attack. Where there's been extensive damage, that person has little ability to defend herself and usually ends up or remains in some kind of bondage.

"Don't they read the Bible and pray?" we might ask. It seems like a reasonable question to most of us.

But we might just as well ask, "Why are some people who go to emergency rooms in agony and bleeding profusely?" The obvious answer is because they've suffered a traumatic, life-threatening injury. Yet no doctor in her right mind would hand such a person a printout of instructions and say, "Now read this every day and pray. If you can't stop bleeding, there's obviously something wrong with your commitment to health. If fact, if you don't stop bleeding pretty soon, you'll no longer be welcome in this hospital!"

Can you imagine such an outrage? Yet suffering saints get this kind of well-meaning counsel from other Christians all the time. Sometimes in my own life, I'm sorry to say, I've either received or given this kind of "spiritual" advice.

Now, believers definitely need to read the Scriptures and pray—that's how our hearts are instructed in the ways of God and how our minds are renewed. But doing a Bible study won't stop the bleeding! Hurting people who belong to the Lord generally don't need to be handed more information. They already read their Bibles and probably own a library full of Christian books. People in pain need to be comforted and healed. They need eye contact, a listening ear, and an encouraging word. They need human touch and Spirit-directed healing prayer into the broken places of their souls. At times they will need to be confronted with truth and encouraged to persevere as they learn to embrace the cross. At other times they need to be gathered in someone's arms, to know that somebody will hang on to them for dear life while they fall apart, and it's all right because God will put them back together.

Yes, an Ezra must come to teach them the laws of God and lead them to repentance. But there must also be a Nehemiah with them down in the dust and rubble of their lives as the hard work of restoration is done.

Did you know that Nehemiah, whose name means "Jehovah has comforted," is a type of the Holy Spirit? Every believer needs the ministry of Nehemiah in his life because every one of us has suffered some damage. That's just the nature of the fall. The Holy Spirit comes to us with great concern and compassion as He surveys the damage in our souls. He never despairs though. He knows exactly what is needed to repair the breaches and restore the gates. If we'll let Him, He'll get right to work alongside us. A lot of healing takes place in our lives as we learn to walk with God because of the ministry of the Holy Spirit to us. That has certainly been my experience. Often, though, we need more than that. We need a Nehemiah with skin on because it takes people to heal people.

I have been blessed to have some "Nehemiahs" in my life. They are the prayer ministers who were brave enough to provoke me to pain to find out why it was there and to pray into it. Several times. And they gave me homework to do and made me an active participant in my own healing. There's the McLean Ministries team that I'm a part of. They have prayed for me on numerous occasions and hung in there with me the day my rage began to uncork.

There's my friend Darline. If I really need to do some serious shopping for clothes, I'll give her a call. I hate to shop for clothes. It is not a recreational activity for me. Because of my old insecurities, it's more like returning to the scene of an accident. I would almost rather take a beating than shop for clothes. Darline, however, is a very patient soul and good moral support, so I'll usually call her when I can't put it off any longer, and online shopping won't suffice. Darline will have extra jewels in her crown because shopping with me was for a while like being with a toddler. I tired easily, said no a lot, and had a very short attention span!

Somewhere between my first visit to Israel and the throes of a profound inner healing, I wrote "The Gates of Zion." It's a fusion of historical events, real-time experience, and prophetic declaration. It's also a very personal prayer for restoration, a hope believed, and a cry for Zion to open the gates to receive the rescue and comfort of her rightful King.

The Gates of Zion

My walls are battered and broken.
My gates have burned to rust.
My wounds are angry and open,
And dreams lie in the dust.
And foreign kings have plundered me,
And dragged away my heart.
But there is a word of prophecy,
The King of love will come to me!

Let the gates of Zion, let the gates of Zion,
Let the gates of Zion be open to You,
Be open to You.

O Lord, You've seen my affliction,
You've heard my cries of fear.

MORE PRECIOUS THAN SILVER

My eyes will see Your salvation.
Redemption's drawing near.
My Shepherd-King, You comfort me,
And wipe away my tears.
There is a word of prophecy,
The King of kings will reign in me!

Let the gates of Zion, let the gates of Zion,
Let the gates of Zion be open to You.

Call out to the holy city,
"Your warfare is through!"
And the Father who loves you, Jerusalem,
Has a double portion for you.

Let the gates of Zion, let the gates of Zion,
Let the gates of Zion be open to You,
Be open to You.

Words and music by Lynn DeShazo
© 2005 Integrity's Hosanna! Music/ASCAP
All rights reserved. Lyrics reprinted by permission.

CHAPTER TWELVE

THERE'S A TABLE

He who eats My flesh and drinks My blood has eternal life,
and I will raise him up on the last day.
For My flesh is true food, and My blood is true drink.
He who eats My flesh and drinks
My blood abides in Me, and I in him.
—John 6:54–56

Iwas totally lost in worship. The more intensely I worshipped the Lord at the women's conference I was attending, the less aware I became of any other person or activity around me. The event was hosted by the Brownsville Assembly of God in Pensacola, Florida, during an outpouring of the Holy Spirit that came to be called the Brownsville Revival. It was 1998, but had you tapped me on the shoulder to inquire, I'm not sure I could have told you that for certain. The presence of the Lord was profoundly manifested to me, and Jesus alone was the focus of my attention and adoration.

Suddenly, I caught a glimpse into the heavenly tabernacle with the eyes of my spirit, as though a door into the Holy Place itself had opened just enough for revelation. Then I heard myself say these words out loud as the revelation dropped into me. "It's about a table! Worship is about a table!" Thus began my odyssey to search out the mystery and meaning of the sacramental act of worship that Christians call Holy Communion.

I've been a regular part of a local church all of my life. Many times have I received the body and the blood, often in the form of a tiny puff of bread and a tiny cup of grape juice. As a child, I was always glad for that bit of juice to wash down the dry little wafer given to us in my Methodist church. Back then, I'm not sure I understood much about why we "took Communion" every few weeks, but I knew it had something to do with Jesus' dying on a cross for our sins. Even children can understand that basic concept, given a little instruction. But that was probably the extent of my own understanding of the Lord's Table for many years. Until, that is, my ministry travels during the 1990s took me to a series of Episcopal churches, where the celebration of the Lord's Table is observed every week.

Most of my invitations to minister have come because of the songs I've written. "Since the song has ministered to us," the logic goes, "perhaps the songwriter can, too." That's the short answer to how I started traveling in ministry. And it's how I ended up on the worship team for an Episcopal renewal conference two summers in a row. And why I got a string of invitations to minister in these churches that celebrated the Lord's Table every Sunday I happened to be with them. Although I came fully prepared to minister in the capacity of a worship leader and a workshop teacher, I soon found myself on the receiving end of ministry. As I participated in the services, I often gazed upon the bread and the cup. Then something happened to me.

In my youth God used the ministry of anointed music to create a hunger in me for His presence. Years later, worshipping in the sanctuaries of a centuries-old denomination, I found a fresh hunger stirring within me to know Him more intimately. Only this time it wasn't the newly created songs of worship that touched me so profoundly. I was the one ministering through music. What stirred my heart so deeply were the ancient symbols of the body and blood of Christ—bread and wine—and the wordless call of the Spirit to Holy Communion. I found myself powerfully drawn to the Communion table from that time on. My understanding and practice of biblical worship began to change and mature, though it would be hard for me to explain in just a few words how that process unfolded.

When spiritual revelation comes to a person, it enlarges one's insight and understanding in the flash of a nanosecond. God opens the eyes of your heart, and you finally understand what you haven't been able to see before. When I experienced my "mini-vision" that day in Pensacola, something heavenly awakened inside me. All that God had been wordlessly speaking to me through the Communion table began to come together in that moment. I was so excited; I just kept saying over and over to myself, "It's about a table! Worship is about a table!" I barely knew what I was talking about, yet I knew I was on to something very significant.

I began devouring everything I could get my hands on about the Lord's Table. I studied the New Testament references. I studied the Passover. I studied ancient Jewish wedding rites and other cultural aspects related to my studies. I highlighted every mention of covenant in my daily Scripture readings. I ordered audio teaching materials on topics like the sacraments and the blood covenant, and I listened to them over and over again. With the passion of a knight in search of the Holy Grail, I leaned as hard as I could into furthering my understanding. I began to use my studies in the ministry opportunities that came my way. In my zeal I even cornered my pastor one Sunday and asked him if he would let me share some of the things I was learning with our church. Graciously, he allowed it. All the while, I continued to grope for understanding. I was like someone in the dark running her fingers across the wall in hopes of finding the light switch, saying, "I know it's here somewhere!"

Is the Lord's Table full of secret, mysterious meaning that will only be revealed to a select few? Far from it. The significance of Jesus' words and actions throughout His ministry were not lost on His Jewish disciples. He came to make the Father known to them, not to obscure Him. The problem is that the church has been so long cut off from the Jewish roots of our faith—the reasons are varied and often tragic—that we haven't been able to reap the nourishing benefits of the olive tree of Israel, which God so carefully grafted us into through Jesus Christ. Because of my inherited loss of understanding, certain cultural expressions of covenant, such as the breaking of bread or the drinking of wine from a cup during a marriage betrothal—so readily understood by ancient Israel—were lost on me when I read the Scriptures.

All my life I'd been trained to see the world through Greek glasses rather than Hebrew ones. Consequently, when I read in Exodus about the table of showbread that stood in the inner court of the tabernacle, I never truly understood its significance. Nor did I fully comprehend David's words in Psalm 23. "You prepare a table before me in the presence of my enemies" (v. 5).

And the list goes on and on.

I think that's why my search took on such intensity. I was straining to overcome a deficit of understanding because the rite had been disconnected from its roots. When the Lord began to enlighten my understanding through the study of these Jewish roots, I felt like I'd made a wonderful, yet tragic discovery. I felt the chagrin of someone invited to the party who'd been satisfied to lick the icing from a birthday candle only to realize that I could have helped myself to several big slices of the cake! The Lord's Table is so rich with meaning to me now that I hardly know where to begin to describe it.

One morning while preparing for a women's retreat on the Lord's Table, I spent some time rereading the passages in Exodus that describe the tabernacle furnishings. God gave His instructions to Moses concerning the wilderness tabernacle in great detail and admonished him to make it exactly according to the pattern shown to him on Mount Sinai. As I reflected on what I read, I considered the order in which God instructed Moses to set up the furnishings of the tabernacle.

> Then the Lord spoke to Moses, saying, "On the first day of the first month you shall set up the tabernacle of the tent of meeting. You shall place the ark of the testimony there, and you shall screen the ark with the veil."
> —Exodus 40:1–3

Going out from the ark sequentially, the next item I expected to read about was the golden altar of incense. But I didn't. Instead God's instruction read,

> You shall bring in the table and arrange what belongs on it.
> —Exodus 40:4a

I'd never noticed that detail before. If the closest physical proximity to the ark was significant, God didn't seem to be making a point of it here, unlike many of the sermons I'd heard on the subject of worship. They tended to emphasize the altar of incense because it stood before the veil, just outside the holy of holies where the ark rested. He goes on.

> And you shall bring in the lampstand and mount its lamps. Moreover, you shall set the gold altar of incense before the ark of the testimony, and set up the veil for the doorway to the tabernacle.
>
> —Exodus 40:4b–5

I pondered the order I'd just read about—the ark, the table, the lampstand, the altar of incense; the ark . . . the table . . . the lampstand . . . the altar of incense . . .

And then I saw it. God wasn't describing a sequence, as we Greek-thinking Gentiles tend to read it. He was painting a picture. And the picture was incredible: *I was looking at a candlelight dinner!* I was so excited that I nearly fell out of my chair! I threw back my head and laughed out loud for sheer joy at the revelation.

Worship really is about a table!

During the time of Moses, the sons of Aaron were commanded to gather around the table of showbread every Sabbath to eat the bread of the presence.[18] They would also burn frankincense from the table upon the altar of incense, the pungent smoke rising as worship before the Most High. What a picture—the priests of the Lord gathered around His table to fellowship with almighty God in the breaking of bread and by their ministry of worship. These hardworking priests were surely energized by eating the bread that had been soaking up the presence of the Lord all week. How much more should believers through the new covenant be spiritually strengthened and nourished by regular communion with our Savior, the true Bread of heaven? I began to see that the celebration of the Lord's Table was not only a sacramental act of worship but also a glorious picture of how we should live our lives—*in Holy Communion* with the Giver, Sustainer, and Redeemer of life; and *in holy community* with one another.

As I continued to reflect on the Lord's Table, I gained a whole new appreciation for how deeply God desires to be with His people. Something was familiar to me about the order God gave Moses for setting up the tabernacle furnishings. I pondered it again. Once more the light of His revelation flooded my heart. I thought, *It's been a while since I've moved, but I always have certain priorities about settling into a new place. The top three are setting up my bed, setting up a dining table, and then plugging in some lamps to get enough light in the place.*

My face became one big grin as I realized what I was reading about. God was preparing to move to a new address—from heaven to earth— *and He was excited about it!* The Glory of Israel was preparing to dwell among His people, and He had essentially the same priorities I did when moving to a new dwelling: *a resting place, a table, and a lamp!*

Before God came down to us in the incarnation, He dwelled with His people in the confines of a tabernacle or temple, always veiled from the view of even the priesthood. Only the high priest could pass beyond the veil to minister before the ark of the testimony with its mercy seat, the symbol to Israel of God's holy presence. When God sent His Son, Jesus became to us the Word made flesh (see John 1:14). The Glory of God humbly walked among His people in the body of Jesus Christ. He was a living, breathing "ark of the testimony."

After the death and resurrection of Jesus, the Holy Spirit was poured out upon the church at Pentecost, and now He inhabits the tabernacle of our bodies. Now *we* are the living, breathing arks, redeemed containers of the glory and Spirit of the Lord! Every believer was meant to live as a worshipping priest, with an open invitation to the table of the Lord. In that place of Holy Communion, we find rest in Him and strength for our souls as we partake of the Bread of Life with gratitude and rejoicing. And in the light of His presence, the love of God is poured out upon our hearts by the Holy Spirit.

Inevitably, the meditations of my heart poured out into song, and I do mean *poured out*. I cowrote "There's a Table" in July 2004 with my friend and fellow songwriter Gary Sadler during the second half of a writing session. We hadn't planned to write on the theme of Communion, but my heart was so full of all the Lord had shown me that the lyrics just spilled out at the first opportunity. Gary's musical ideas were an exquisite match, and the result was a hauntingly beautiful piece of music that I am still very proud of.

Every Sabbath, as they've done for thousands of years, Jewish families gather around a table as the sun sets, and offer prayers to God as bread is broken and the fruit of the vine enjoyed. Around this table, fathers speak a blessing over their children and openly praise their wives. It is a joyful time of resting from one's labors while observing the Lord's commandment to keep the Sabbath day holy. At the consummation of the ages, the sun will set for the last time on this closing era and the day of the Lord will begin—the true Sabbath that all others are but a shadow of. We who are the bride of Christ and the family of God will joyfully gather around His banquet table for the great marriage supper of the Lamb (Rev. 19:1–9). Until that blessed time, we have this charge from the Lord: "Do this in remembrance of Me" (Luke 22:19). And in doing so, we "proclaim the Lord's death until He comes" (1 Cor. 11:26).

Maranatha! Come, Lord Jesus.

There's a Table

There's a table in Your Presence,
Where the weary are restored,
Where the bread is broken for us,
And the cup of life is poured.

Blood and body given for us,
Perfect offering for our sin.
Sacrifice and resurrection,
All who die with You shall live.

Hallelujah, hallelujah!
Worthy is the Lamb of God!
Maranatha, maranatha!
Lord of our salvation, come!

God our Father, Christ our Savior,
To Your table now we come.
In this holy, sweet communion,
Fill our hearts and make us one.

Hallelujah, hallelujah!
Worthy is the Lamb of God!
Maranatha, maranatha!
Lord of our salvation, come!

Words and music by Lynn DeShazo and Gary Sadler
© 2005 Integrity's Hosanna! Music and Paintbrush Music

CHAPTER THIRTEEN

MERCY'S SACRIFICE

God is humble.

—Mother Teresa

I have enjoyed making music and singing for as long as I can remember. My mother tells me I was fond of standing on a footstool as a toddler and singing commercial jingles as they played on the television. One of my dad's favorite Christmas stories of me was the year my parents gave me a Mickey Mouse toy guitar. The little guitar played tunes as you turned the handle around and around. I was a blur, he tells me, as I ran excitedly back and forth among the guitar, the cowboy outfit, and the doll that were all under the Christmas tree for me that year. As it turned out, that little guitar would be the first of several he would pay for over the course of my musical education.

I was too young to remember either of my parents' stories myself, but most of my own best childhood memories are also connected to music. I remember listening to my older cousins' 45-rpm records and singing along to songs like "Charlie Brown" by the Coasters and the Kingston Trio's "The Ballad of the MTA."

Once I started learning to play guitar, I spent hours listening to the radio and picking out favorite songs. I made up funny ones or wrote parodies of popular songs for the amusement of my friends. There were all my moments of musical discovery, such as learning a new chord—ooohh, listen to that major seventh!—or getting to borrow an older friend's Sears

Silvertone electric guitar. The hard case was also the amplifier, and how cool was that? Or the day I figured out I could use a spray deodorant can to simulate the sound of a slide guitar. Then there was my collection of Hohner harmonicas and trying to play like Neil Young on "Heart of Gold." Or hearing my own voice on tape for the first time. Ad infinitum.

As a young songwriter and musician, I was of course much enamored of music. Most young people are, I suppose. When I discovered how powerful worshipping God with music could be, I was never the same. In my young mind, worshipping God became equivalent to worshipping with music, particularly if it was the music I preferred. I would eventually learn, however, that some of the greatest acts of worship found in the Bible occurred without the accompaniment of pipe organ, choir, or guitar.

> Now it came about after these things, that God tested Abraham, and said to him, "Abraham!"
>
> And he said, "Here I am."
>
> "Take now your son, your only son, whom you love, Isaac, and go to the land of Moriah, and offer him there as a burnt offering on one of the mountains of which I will tell you."
> —Genesis 22:1–2

Gulp!
"Yes, Lord."
This, of course, is the familiar beginning of the account known to Jewish scholars as the *Akedah* or the binding of Isaac, one of the most extraordinary events recorded in the Scriptures. What has always impressed me about this passage, however, is what we *don't* read there.

I can only imagine what must have gone through Abraham's mind. He had waited twenty years for Isaac, the heir that God had promised would issue from his and Sarah's own aged bodies. Now he was being asked to do the unthinkable—to sacrifice the beloved son who was the fulfillment of all those years they had stood in faith and believed God. Amazingly, no protest from Abraham is noted in Genesis 22, no Bedouin bargaining. "Lord, you know Sarah's getting on up there in age. What about her instead of Isaac?" Nothing like that crossed Abraham's lips. We see no refusal or angry fist raised to the heavens either. We see only the story of a man hearing the voice of God and then fully obeying what he was told to do. The Bible calls that *worship*.

> So Abraham rose early in the morning and saddled his donkey, and took two of his young men with him and Isaac his son; and he split wood for the burnt offering, and arose and went to the place of which God had told him. On the third day Abraham raised his eyes and saw the place from a distance. Abraham said to his young men, "Stay here with the donkey, and I and the lad will go over there; and we will worship and return to you."
>
> —Genesis 22:3–5

To Abraham's great relief, God was only testing him. The Lord wanted to see if Abraham really feared Him and if he would hold anything back, even his only son. There wasn't. He passed his test of trust in God's covenant with flying colors, as we say, and blessed the world by his obedience (see Gen. 22:18).

Thankfully, Abraham's heartrending pilgrimage ended well. His beloved son was restored to him, and another died in his place. God Himself provided the lamb for Abraham's sacrifice that day; a ram was found nearby with its head caught in a thicket of thorns. What a beautiful picture of the time, still far beyond this patriarch of faith, when the Son of God would wear a crown of thorns about His head and die a sacrificial, atoning death for the sins of the world! God would not withhold His only Son either.

About two thousand years after Abraham, the Lamb of God would suffer at the hands of the ones He came to save, both Jews and Gentiles. Jesus would be arrested, falsely accused, cruelly humiliated, and beaten beyond recognition. He would be stripped naked, subjected to a brutal Roman scourging, and then have a crown of thorns shoved down on His head—a mockery of His true claim to the throne of David. Like Isaac, He would carry the wood for the sacrifice Himself to the place of His death and then be violently nailed upon that cross through His hands and feet. Jesus would suffer all these horrors willingly and without a word of protest or complaint. He would give to God, His Father, the most perfect offering of worship ever given by anyone in any time or in any place—His very own life laid down. Now all who believe in Him, as the Bible says, "shall not perish, but have eternal life" (see John 3:16).

The Bible, of course, has a lot to say about the musical expression of praise and worship. After all, the 150 psalms are found right in the middle of it. Jesus Himself sang from them often, including the very night of His betrayal and arrest.[19] The proof of true worship, though, is a life laid down in obedience to the God one claims to worship. No finer example of a true worshipper exists in all of human history than Jesus.

Learning to worship God is a lesson in humility. There is simply no place for pride in the presence of the One who is Himself not proud.[20] Absolutely nothing we can say about ourselves would either impress Him with our accomplishments or discourage Him from wanting to be near us. We can do nothing to earn His pleasure. He just loves us! At the same time, He is holy. More than anything else, God is *holy,* and His holiness would absolutely destroy the sin and corruption in us if we got anywhere near Him. (This is why God veiled Himself from Israel within the confines of the tabernacle or temple until the time was right for Jesus to come into the world as our Savior. The veil was for their own good!) But God is also humble; when we couldn't come to Him because of our sinful condition, He came to us—as one of us—and gave His life to redeem ours.

> Have this attitude in yourselves which was also in Christ Jesus, who, although He existed in the form of God, did not regard equality with God a thing to be grasped, but emptied Himself, taking the form of a bond-servant, and being made in the likeness of men. Being found in appearance as a man, He humbled Himself by becoming obedient to the point of death, even death on a cross.
>
> —Philippians 2:5–8

Honestly, I have known the story of Jesus for so long that I sometimes forget just how astonishing it truly is. God humbled Himself! The very idea is so extraordinary that I cannot wrap my mind around it. I'll never be able to fully comprehend the magnitude of what He has done for me or the greatness of His gift of salvation. I can only accept it with deep gratitude and continually praise Him for it! That's why I'm still writing songs for worship to this day.

Interestingly, it's the familiarity of the story that makes it so challenging to write about. One day, while going through a pile of lyric ideas, I came upon one that focused on the cross. As I read it, I was reminded of the trouble I had satisfactorily shaping the idea and of why it was still lying on my desk gathering dust! I'd been straining to write a theological masterpiece, a song that might be deemed a great hymn of the church one day. Only I wasn't doing it very successfully. So I decided to abandon my quest for a "hymn hit" and start over. I then focused on writing my version of "the greatest story every told" the way I do it best, which is simply.

I wrote four verses, which I loved, and a very convoluted bridge section I knew wouldn't work at all. So in a cowriting session with Michael Neale at his office at The People's Church in Franklin, Tennessee, I asked him if he had any ideas. He did, and the result was a much better bridge melody. Great! I would live with the song for a while and see if I needed to change anything else before I called it "done."

While in Franklin, I had also written with Gary Sadler earlier in the week. I recorded a rough demo of "Mercy's Sacrifice" at Gary's house before I headed for home, and he made a brilliant observation. I sang the first line of the bridge: "And I am forgiven, and love is mine." Gary listened attentively and said, "You ought to change that to 'all is forgiven.'"

Bingo! He was absolutely right. I like to think that I would have come up with that idea on my own, given a few more days of mulling it over. But who knows for sure? Thanks for the suggestion, Gary. And thanks be to God for His indescribable gift!

Mercy's Sacrifice

Crown of thorns, body torn,
Abused and left to die.
Tender man, God's own Lamb,
Mercy's sacrifice.

Humble King suffering,
For crimes that I have done.

MORE PRECIOUS THAN SILVER

Nail and scourge, justice served,
By mercy's sacrifice.

And all is forgiven, and love is mine.
What a beautiful gift I've been given,
By mercy's sacrifice.

Gift of grace, God's own face,
And heaven open wide.
Evil one overcome,
By mercy's sacrifice.

And all is forgiven, and love is mine.
What a beautiful gift I've been given,
By mercy's sacrifice.

Majesty serving me,
With hands held out in love.
So I run to You and fall into,
The everlasting arms.

And all is forgiven, and love is mine.
What a beautiful gift I've been given,
By mercy's sacrifice.

ENDNOTES

1. Chuck Girard and others, lyrics, "Praise the Lord," Dunamis Music, 1972.

2. From the Liturgy of "The Holy Eucharist: Rite Two," *The Book of Common Prayer*.

3. Laura B. Randolph, "The Lady and the Champ," *Ebony*, February 1997, 74.

4. Read more about Wycliffe Bible Translators at http://www.wycliffe.org. For information about Wycliffe Canada, go to http://www.wycliffe.ca.

5. A. Kenneth Curtis, J. Stephen Lang, and Randy Petersen, *The 100 Most Important Events in Christian History* (Grand Rapids, MI: Baker/Revell, 1998), 87.

6. Sheila Davis, *The Craft of Lyric Writing* (Cincinnati, OH: Writer's Digest Books, 1984), 7.

7. James H. Ferguson, D.C.E., *The Book of Ephesians Course Study Guide* syllabus (Columbus, GA: Christian Life School of Theology), 32.

8. Refer to Ephesians 6:12.

9. Jamie Owens-Collins, "The Battle Belongs to the Lord," Fairhill Music, 1985.

10. Bunny never dreamed that the eulogy she penned would ever appear in published form. She wrote it in the wake of her grief, and only for family and friends. She has graciously given me her permission to reprint it.

11. Do you know a woman who needs the ministry of Wellspring for Women? Contact the organization at www.wellspringforwomen. org. Would you like to help Wellspring for Women? Consider sending a donation in memory of Ms. Ev or your own loved one. Please make your check payable to: Wellspring for Women, 2377 County Road 65, Marbury, AL 36067.

12. Refer to 1 Corinthians 12:31.

13. Richard Booker, PhD., *"Jerusalem, The Eternal," Restore!* Peace of Jerusalem issue, 26.

14. Refer to Leviticus 26.

15. Refer to Deuteronomy 29:14–28; 2 Kings 17.

16. Refer to Jeremiah 39:10.

17. Refer to Ezra.

18. Refer to Leviticus 24:5–9.

19. Refer to Matthew 26:30.

20. Refer to Matthew 11:29.

AUTHOR'S NOTE

I've written hundreds of songs in the course of thirty years. About 17 percent of them have been recorded by Integrity Music. I couldn't begin to tell you how many other record companies or independent artists have recorded these songs. Another 15 percent or so have been recorded by me. Every one of them has some kind of story behind it.

Not every song has a story that's substantial enough to write about though, like "Stand Up and Give Him the Praise," which is actually a fairly well-known song of mine. About the only story behind this song is that I was trying to write for a Ron Kenoly project, a popular artist with Integrity Music at the time. My tune didn't make it to Ron's recording; Paul Wilbur actually recorded the song. Integrity Music released it in 1995 on a project called *Shalom Jerusalem*. From there, it took on a life of its own.

Eric Nuzum, the worship leader for a small church in Smithton, Missouri (population 532), happened to be leading the congregation in "Stand Up and Give Him the Praise" during a March evening service in 1996 when the power of God hit the church. It started with their pastor, Steve Gray, who was so discouraged in his life and ministry that he had almost thrown in the towel. Instead, God threw a big revival in that tiny midwestern town, and over two hundred and fifty thousand people visited the church over a three-year period! As a result of their experience, "Stand Up and Give Him the Praise" came to be closely associated with the revival. I love that one of my songs had a significant role in the story of the Smithton Outpouring, but it's still *their* story.

I have chosen to write about songs that not only have a story worth telling, in my estimation, but also tell a part of *my* story. Just as there's a story behind every song, there's one behind every songwriter. This book is not intended to be a complete autobiography though. Think of it as a song memoir of sorts. Or maybe just a collection of inspiring and sometimes humorous snapshots of one woman's walk of faith—and keep in mind that I'm still on the journey!

I am also keenly aware that several of my songs have become very meaningful to a wide cross section of the body of Christ. That is a high honor for me, and I am very grateful for the privilege of having served the Lord's people in this way. It is still the greatest of compliments to hear someone say to me, "You wrote what I wanted to say to the Lord!"

> My heart overflows with a good theme; I address my verses
> to the King; my tongue is the pen of a ready writer.
> —Psalm 45:1

Do you have a story about how God has touched your life through one of Lynn's songs? She'd love to hear from you! Contact her at http://www.lynndeshazo.com or write to Lynn DeShazo, Ready Writer Music, PO Box 43097, Birmingham, AL 35243.

To buy additional copies of this book or to find the songs Lynn wrote about, go to http://www.lynndeshazo.com. Get discounted shipping with this coupon code: SHIPDISC.

To order additional copies of this book call:
1-877-421-READ (7323)
or please visit our Web site at
www.winepressbooks.com

If you enjoyed this quality custom-published book,
drop by our Web site for more books and information.

www.winepressgroup.com

"Your partner in custom publishing."